MACMILLAN MASTER GUIDES

GREAT EXPECTATIONS

BY CHARLES DICKENS

DENNIS BUTTS

MACMILLAN

First published 1985 by
THE MACMILLAN PRESS LTD
Houndmills, Basingstoke, Hampshire RG21 2XS
and London
Companies and representatives
throughout the world

ISBN 0–333–37427–4

A catalogue record for this book is available
from the British Library.

Reprinted 1992, 1993, 1994

Printed in Malaysia

MASTER GUIDES

GENERAL EDITOR: JAMES GIBSON

JANE AUSTEN	*Emma* Norman Page
	Sense and Sensibility Judy Simons
	Persuasion Judy Simons
	Pride and Prejudice Raymond Wilson
	Mansfield Park Richard Wirdnam
SAMUEL BECKETT	*Waiting for Godot* Jennifer Birkett
WILLIAM BLAKE	*Songs of Innocence and Songs of Experience*
	Alan Tomlinson
ROBERT BOLT	*A Man for All Seasons* Leonard Smith
CHARLOTTE BRONTË	*Jane Eyre* Robert Miles
EMILY BRONTË	*Wuthering Heights* Hilda D. Spear
JOHN BUNYAN	*The Pilgrim's Progress* Beatrice Batson
GEOFFREY CHAUCER	*The Miller's Tale* Michael Alexander
	The Pardoner's Tale Geoffrey Lester
	The Wife of Bath's Tale Nicholas Marsh
	The Knight's Tale Anne Samson
	The Prologue to the Canterbury Tales
	Nigel Thomas and Richard Swan
JOSEPH CONRAD	*The Secret Agent* Andrew Mayne
CHARLES DICKENS	*Bleak House* Dennis Butts
	Great Expectations Dennis Butts
	Hard Times Norman Page
GEORGE ELIOT	*Middlemarch* Graham Handley
	Silas Marner Graham Handley
	The Mill on the Floss Helen Wheeler
T. S. ELIOT	*Murder in the Cathedral* Paul Lapworth
	Selected Poems Andrew Swarbrick
HENRY FIELDING	*Joseph Andrews* Trevor Johnson
E. M. FORSTER	*A Passage to India* Hilda D. Spear
	Howards End Ian Milligan
WILLIAM GOLDING	*The Spire* Rosemary Sumner
	Lord of the Flies Raymond Wilson
OLIVER GOLDSMITH	*She Stoops to Conquer* Paul Ranger
THOMAS HARDY	*The Mayor of Casterbridge* Ray Evans
	Tess of the d'Urbervilles James Gibson
	Far from the Madding Crowd
	Colin Temblett-Wood
BEN JONSON	*Volpone* Michael Stout
JOHN KEATS	*Selected Poems* John Garrett
RUDYARD KIPLING	*Kim* Leonée Ormond
PHILIP LARKIN	*The Less Deceived* and *The Whitsun Weddings*
	Andrew Swarbrick

D.H. LAWRENCE	*Sons and Lovers* R. P. Draper
HARPER LEE	*To Kill a Mockingbird* Jean Armstrong
LAURIE LEE	*Cider with Rosie* Brian Tarbitt
GERARD MANLEY HOPKINS	*Selected Poems* R. J. C. Watt
CHRISTOPHER MARLOWE	*Doctor Faustus* David A. Male
THE METAPHYSICAL POETS	Joan van Emden
THOMAS MIDDLETON and WILLIAM ROWLEY	*The Changeling* Tony Bromham
ARTHUR MILLER	*The Crucible* Leonard Smith *Death of a Salesman* Peter Spalding
GEORGE ORWELL	*Animal Farm* Jean Armstrong
WILLIAM SHAKESPEARE	*Richard II* Charles Barber *Othello* Tony Bromham *Hamlet* Jean Brooks *King Lear* Francis Casey *Henry V* Peter Davison *The Winter's Tale* Diana Devlin *Julius Caesar* David Elloway *Macbeth* David Elloway *The Merchant of Venice* A. M. Kinghorn *Measure for Measure* Mark Lilly *Henry IV Part I* Helen Morris *Romeo and Juliet* Helen Morris *A Midsummer Night's Dream* Kenneth Pickering *The Tempest* Kenneth Pickering *Coriolanus* Gordon Williams *Antony and Cleopatra* Martin Wine *Twelfth Night* R. P. Draper
GEORGE BERNARD SHAW	*St Joan* Leonée Ormond
RICHARD SHERIDAN	*The School for Scandal* Paul Ranger *The Rivals* Jeremy Rowe
ALFRED TENNYSON	*In Memoriam* Richard Gill
EDWARD THOMAS	*Selected Poems* Gerald Roberts
ANTHONY TROLLOPE	*Barchester Towers* K. M. Newton
JOHN WEBSTER	*The White Devil* and *The Duchess of Malfi* David A. Male
VIRGINIA WOOLF	*To the Lighthouse* John Mepham *Mrs Dalloway* Julian Pattison
WILLIAM WORDSWORTH	*The Prelude Books I and II* Helen Wheeler

CONTENTS

GENERAL EDITOR'S PREFACE

The aim of the Macmillan Master Guides is to help you to appreciate the book you are studying by providing information about it and by suggesting ways of reading and thinking about it which will lead to a fuller understanding. The section on the writer's life and background has been designed to illustrate those aspects of the writer's life which have influenced the work, and to place it in its personal and literary context. The summaries and critical commentary are of special importance in that each brief summary of the action is followed by an examination of the significant critical points. The space which might have been given to repetitive explanatory notes has been devoted to a detailed analysis of the kind of passage which might confront you in an examination. Literary criticism is concerned with both the broader aspects of the work being studied and with its detail. The ideas which meet us in reading a great work of literature, and their relevance to us today, are an essential part of our study, and our Guides look at the thought of their subject in some detail. But just as essential is the craft with which the writer has constructed his work of art, and this is considered under several technical headings -- characterisation, language, style and stagecraft.

The authors of these Guides are all teachers and writers of wide experience, and they have chosen to write about books they admire and know well in the belief that they can communicate their admiration to you. But you yourself must read and know intimately the book you are studying. No one can do that for you. You should see this book as a lamppost. Use it to shed light, not to lean against. If you know your text and know what it is saying about life, and how it says it, then you will enjoy it, and there is no better way of passing an examination in literature.

JAMES GIBSON

ACKNOWLEDGEMENTS

Cover illustration: *A Country Blacksmith Disputing Upon The Price of Iron* by Turner, courtesy of the Tate Gallery.

x

1 CHARLES DICKENS: LIFE AND BACKGROUND

Charles Dickens was born on 7th February 1812, in Landport, a district of Portsmouth, where his father John Dickens worked as a clerk in the Navy Pay Office. In 1817 the family moved to Chatham near the river Medway in Kent where Charles enjoyed a happy childhood in the region of Rochester and the surrounding riverside and country of the marshes.

Mr Dickens moved to work in London in 1882, but he was not very prudent financially and his fortunes declined so much that he was sent to prison for debt. What followed shattered young Charles. He was taken away from school and sent to work in Warren's Blacking Warehouse at Hungerford Stairs in London, and though the distressing experience only lasted a few months it left an indelible impression of shame and bitterness on the young boy's mind. The impression of being totally abandoned in the world was so powerful that Dickens could rarely bring himself to speak of it, even in later years when he was rich and famous. (This experience perhaps explains Joe's visit to the Ware'us in Chapter 27 of the novel.)

A few months later Mr Dickens was discharged from prison and obtained work again, so he was able to rescue Charles from the Warehouse and send him back to school. Here he read widely, particularly translations of *Don Quixote* and of *The Arabian Nights*, and such eighteenth-century English novels as *Tom Jones* and *The Vicar of Wakefield*. At school he also acquired his lifelong interest in drama.

After leaving school at the age of fifteen in 1827 Dickens was employed in a solicitor's office, where he obtained many insights into lawyers and the ways of the legal profession, but he taught himself shorthand and then became a newspaper reporter. By 1831 he had become a Parliamentary Reporter and gradually built up a considerable reputation for the speed and excellence of his work. His attendance at Parliamentary debates and political meetings gave him considerable insight into the social problems of the day, the poverty, the social unrest, and all the difficulties occasioned by the Industrial Revolution which later led historians of this period to call it the Bleak Age. Dickens also began to doubt whether Parliament could ever deal with these problems in any satisfactory kind of way.

At the same time as working as a Parliamentary Reporter, Dickens also began writing short stories and sketches, mainly about the people and places of London, for various magazines and newspapers, and in 1836 a collection of these short pieces was published under a pseudonym as *Sketches by 'Boz'*. (Dickens had a younger brother nicknamed Moses and this became corrupted to 'Boses' and then 'Boz,' the name Dickens eventually borrowed.)

One of the leading publishing companies of the day, Chapman and Hall, were so impressed by *Sketches by 'Boz'* that they commissioned its young author to write the letterpress to accompany a series of comic pictures dealing with a club of sporting characters which were to be drawn by a well-known artist, Robert Seymour. They were to appear in monthly instalments costing a shilling each, and the publishers though that they might sell as many as 400 copies a month. Under Dickens's dominant genius, however, the writing became more important than the illustrations, and when Seymour, who had been suffering from depression, committed suicide, he was replaced by a young illustrator Hablôt K. Browne, who used the pseudonym 'Phiz' to harmonise with Dickens's 'Boz'. Thus came about the successful partnership that made *The Posthumous Papers of the Pickwick Club* famous. The depiction of such comic characters as Mr Pickwick and his faithful servant Sam Weller, and such glorious scenes as Mr Pickwick's prosecution by the shady lawyers Dodson and Fogg, helped raise the sales of the novel to about 40 000 a month, and set Dickens off on the start of a long career as England's most popular novelist.

Though *The Pickwick Papers* is mainly a comic novel, there are sombre episodes within it including several scenes set in prison. Dickens's next novel *Oliver Twist* (1837-9) concentrated more on the harsher aspects of life with its powerful indictment of poverty and the treatment of the underprivileged in the early nineteenth century. *Nicholas Nickleby* (1838-9) exhibits both satire in its depiction of the ignorant schoolmaster Mr Squeers, and compassion in its portrait of Smike, the abandoned schoolboy. *The Old Curiosity Shop* of 1840-1 was one of Dickens's greatest successes, and it seemed as if the whole country held its breath as it waited to see what would happen to the young heroine, in much the same way as followers of soap operas today become involved in the lives of their characters. *Barnaby Rudge* (1841), the tale of riots in eighteenth-century London, followed, and in 1843 *A Christmas Carol*, with its depiction of Ebenezer Scrooge, the archetypal miser, proved one of the most popular of all Dickens's works.

By 1840's he was the most successful writer in the English-speaking world. A married man with a growing family whom he loved to entertain with elaborate parties, he visited America in 1842 and later wrote a novel

Martin Chuzzlewit (1843-4) incorporating some of his experiences there. A keen amateur actor, from the 1840s Dickens also began to appear regularly in productions of plays by such writers as Shakespeare and Ben Jonson, the public performances usually given to raise money for charity. As if not busy enough with the writing of such novels as *David Copperfield* (1849-50), Dickens also found time to begin a new weekly magazine *Household Words* in 1850, which involved him in much editorial work, but even so his novel-writing continued unabated. *Bleak House*, in which Dickens uses the device of a detective story to explore the 'Condition of England', appeared in 1852-3, *Hard Times*, a devastating critique of utilitarianism, in 1854, *Little Dorrit* in 1855-7, and *A Tale of Two Cities*, a story about the French Revolution, in 1859.

Since 1853, furthermore, Dickens had occasionally given readings from his novels to raise money for charity, and from 1858 he began a series of over 400 public readings which continued for the rest of his life. A superb mimic, he attracted huge audiences to his readings of comic scenes such as the trial of Mr Pickwick, or pathetic ones such as the death of Paul from *Dombey and Son* (1846-8). His reading of the brutal murder of Nancy by Bill Sikes in *Oliver Twist* was particularly sensational and absolutely shattered his audiences.

Indeed the main reason for Dickens's long and successful career as a novelist seems to lie in this extraordinary ability to combine powerful, vivid and amusing story-telling with the capacity to make serious comments about life, especially its harsh economic realities, the cruelties of many Victorian legal and educational institutions, and the ways in which society's greed for money and the injustices of the class system blighted lives for many, and did little to protect the poor and deprived. In the early novels, such as *Pickwick Papers* and *Oliver Twist*, Dickens was not always able to integrate the diverse elements of his books into unified entities, but one of the most remarkable features of his wholly remarkable career is the way in which from the 1840s onwards he was with growing mastery able to combine popular and serious concerns, so that he could use comic characters or sensational incidents to make serious points. *Great Expectations* is a superb example.

As well as showing a greater control and unity, Dickens's novels from the 1850s also became more sombre in tone. The early novels, such as *Oliver Twist* and *Nicholas Nickleby* were written at a time when conditions were appalling, and Dickens denounced them mercilessly. But there seems to be a buoyancy, even an optimism, about these early books, as if Dickens believed that, though conditions were so dreadful, passionate denunciation would change them. Poverty, workhouses, bad schools could be abolished; society and the law could be reformed. Paradoxically, however, as material conditions began to improve for many people in the 1850s, Dickens's novels seem to become less optimistic, as if he felt that an improvement in living conditions was not enough, and feared that the human spirit itself was in danger of being crushed by forces against which the individual had to struggle to retain any decent integrity.

The immediate origins of *Great Expectations* are well known. In his great biography of Dickens, his friend John Forster recounts how in 1860 Dickens wrote: 'For a little piece I have been writing – or am writing: for I hope to finish it today – such a very fine, new, and grotesque idea has opened upon me, that I begin to doubt whether I had not better cancel the little paper, and reserve the notion for a new book. But it so opens out before *me* that I can see the whole of a serial revolving on it, in a most singular and comic manner.'

Dickens evidently went on revolving in his mind this 'new, and grotesque idea', presumable the idea of Pip's expectations coming from a convict, for some time, and then events forced his hand. During 1860 the sales of his weekly magazine *All The Year Round* (the successor to *Household Words*) were falling off due to the lack of popularity of its current serial, *A Day's Ride* by Charles Lever. 'I called a council of war at the office on Tuesday,' Dickens told Forster in October. 'It was perfectly clear that the one thing to be done was, for me to strike in. I have therefore decided to begin the story as of the length of the *Tale of Two Cities* on the first of December. . .The name is GREAT EXPECTATIONS. I think a good name?'

Though the book's immediate origins are so clear, it is not too difficult to identify other experiences that may also have contributed to the final work. As a small boy, Dickens was often taken by his father to look at a large house at Gad's Hill near Rochester, and when the house came up for sale he was able to buy it and made it his permanent home in 1860. It is only a few miles from Chatham and the Medway towns where Dickens grew up, from Cooling near Gravesend with its thirteen small tombstones for the children of one family, and from Rochester itself where an old house called Restoration House seems to have suggested Miss Havisham's residence. Professor Harry Stone has suggested, furthermore, that memories of eccentric ladies had haunted Dickens's mind for some time, and that an article about the death of one rich old woman, who dressed in white and lived the life of a recluse, appeared in his *Household Narrative* as early as 1850, and Professor Stone also points out that her body was found in York Place only a few hundred feet from the Blacking Warehouse where Dickens had worked as a boy. Some readers have also seen Pip's relationship with Estella of mirroring to some extent Dickens's own relationship with the young actress Ellen Ternan whom he met and fell in love with in 1857. (Indeed the name Estella may be an unconscious echo of Ellen's full name, Ellen Lawless Ternan.)

Great Expectations, then, is a very personal novel in many ways. Set in

London and the Kent of Dickens's boyhood, it teels a story about someone growing up, experiencing happiness and unhappiness; it is about love and success and failure, and it is about changing. It is about someone looking back on his life from middle age and trying to understand what has made him the kind of person he has become. But in telling Pip's story, Dickens is telling a story about the way everyone's character is the result of interactions between environment and personality. In this way Pip's story is the story of everyone.

Its serialisation soon helped to improve the sales of *All The Year Round*, and when the story was published in book form later in 1861 it went into a fourth edition within weeks of its appearance.

Though his health began to fail, Dickens finished one more full-length novel *Our Mutual Friend* (1864-5) and completed an immensely successful series of readings in America in 1867-8, but he collapsed while working on his last novel *The Mystery of Edwin Drood* and died at Gad's Hill on 9th June, 1870.

2 SUMMARIES AND CRITICAL COMMENTARY

2.1 OVERALL SUMMARY OF THE PLOT

First Stage – Chapters 1-19

Pip Pirrip, the narrator of *Great Expectations*, lives on the marshes with his sister and brother-in-law, Joe Gargery, who is the village blacksmith, as his parents and other relations are all dead. One day when the seven-year-old Pip visits the churchyard where his parents and brothers are buried, an escaped convict seizes him, and threatens him with terrible consequences unless Pip gets him a file and some food, which the terrified boy steals from his sister and brother-in-law. Though the escaped convict is soon recaptured, Pip never forgets this early alarm or the way it made him steal from and deceive Joe and his sister.

When he grows older, Pip is employed by a rich, eccentric lady, Miss Havisham, to play with her adopted ward, and, though Estella treats Pip with contempt, he admires her for her beauty and self-possession, and falls in love with her. (Pip learns later that Miss Havisham's eccentric behaviour is caused by the fact that she was abandoned on her wedding day by her fiancé, Compeyson, years earlier.) Though Pip had looked forward to becoming Joe's apprentice in the village forge, his acquaintance with Estella and the way she despises his lowly origins makes him ashamed of himself, and he longs to become a gentleman. One day Pip's sister, Mrs Joe, is brutally assaulted, and though Pip suspects Joe's journeyman, Orlick, there is no proof. Pip's former teacher, Biddy, moves into Joe's house to nurse Mrs Joe. Then, in a remarkable change of fortune, Pip learns from a lawyer, Mr Jaggers, that he has 'great expectations,' and should leave the marshes to begin to learn the life of a gentlemen. Believing that the source of his wealth is Miss Havisham, Pip leaves Joe and Biddy and sets out for London.

Second Stage – Chapters 20–39

Pip settles into lodgings in London with Herbert Pocket, under the tuition of whose father he gradually acquires the good manners of a gentleman, but also indulges in extravagance and becomes rather snobbish, being particularly embarrassed by a visit Joe makes to him. Estella grows into a beautiful young woman and Pip loves her more than ever, though his love is not really reciprocated, and Pip is dismayed by her growing relationship with his boorish acquaintance, Bentley Drummle. Just after his twenty-third birthday, late one stormy evening Pip is visited by a stranger whom he recognises as the convict he helped on the marshes when he was a small boy. The stranger named Magwitch, reveals that he prospered after being transported to Australia, and that *he* is Pip's secret benefactor, not Miss Havisham.

Third Stage – Chapters 40–59

Pip is shattered by the discovery of the identity of his secret benefactor. Not only does he dislike the convict's coarse behaviour, but he is dismayed by the knowledge that the source of his great expectations is a criminal, not Miss Havisham, and that she had no plan for him to marry Estella. Pip learns that Estella has married Bentley Drummle, in fact. However, as Pip becomes more aware of Magwitch's sad history, particularly the way he was tricked by his one-time accomplice Compeyson, he is moved to pity him, and resolves to prevent his being punished for returning to England from Australia. With Herbert's help he plans to row Magwitch down the river Thames and put him on a boat to Hamburg, but, though Pip manages to escape from a brutal assault from Orlick, the police arrest Magwitch, after a fight in which Compeyson is killed, and he dies in prison shortly afterwards, deeply loved by the Pip who had once despised him.

Pip is exhausted by his efforts and falls seriously ill, until nursed back to health by Joe. Pip returns to the marshes to ask Joe's forgiveness for his ingratitude, and to propose to Biddy. Too late Pip discovers that she has married Joe. Pip goes abroad and works for his friend Herbert for eleven years, and when he returns to England he finds Joe and Biddy with two young children, their boy being the image of young Pip. When Pip revisits Miss Havisham's old house, he finds that it has been destroyed, but that Estella, now widowed, is walking in the garden. Hand in hand, they leave the garden together.

2.2 CHAPTER SUMMARIES AND CRITICAL COMMENTARY

Chapter 1

Summary

Pip Pirrip, the narrator of the story, lives with his sister, Mrs Joe Gargery, wife of the blacksmith, as his parents and brothers are all dead and buried in the local churchyard in the marsh country. Late one Christmas Eve, when Pip visits the churchyard, a frightening stranger seizes him, and threatens him with terrible consequences at the hands of a friendly 'young man', unless Pip gets him a file to remove his leg-iron, and some food. Pip promises to do so and runs home.

Commentary

This is a brilliant opening chapter, immediately gripping the reader's attention with the dramatic plight of the young boy and his confrontation with the frightening adult. At once a number of narrative questions are raised: who exactly is the stranger? Will Pip return to the churchyard – and what will happen then? Psychologically, the chapter tells us a good deal about Pip, emphasising his loneliness and his imaginative fancies about his dead relatives, with his sense of insecurity perhaps reinforced by the fact that his full name is almost lost! Though Magwitch is mainly presented as a frightening character at this stage, there are plenty of signs that he is to be pitied, too, for his desperate physical condition. The chapter is not without humour, in Pip's musings about his dead family from the appearance of their tombstones, and in the extravagant, cannibalistic threats of the runaway convict, but even these comic references help to show how harsh and violent is Pip's world. Death and violence are never far away. The sky is angry, and the monotony of the landscape is broken only by an ugly beacon and a gibbet. Even the church seems to turn upside down momentarily, as if to suggest its helplessness. Pip imagines he sees the hands of dead people clutching at the stranger as he leaves the churchyard, and this is the first reference to hands, which are to become a recurring image in the novel.

Chapter 2

Summary

Pip runs home to his sister and brother-in-law, Joe, and his sister punishes him for being absent. At tea he steals some bread and butter for the stranger, and is dosed with tar-water because he is thought to have bolted his food. Guns are heard signalling the escape of another convict from the Hulks of a prison-ship. In the early light of next day Pip steals some food and a file from Joe's forge, and takes them to the marshes.

Commentary

Though Pip enjoys the company of kindly Joe Gargery, his brother-in-law is not able to protect him from his sister's physical torments, nor the way she constantly tries to make him feel guilty for not behaving better in gratitude for his upbringing. The almost continual feelings of inadequacy induced in Pip by his sister are now increased, not only by his fear of the convict, but by the knowledge that he has become a thief and robbed his sister to help him. In the portrait of Mrs Joe, Dickens reveals her severe character, partly by his description of her 'hard and heavy hand', another use of such references in the novel. Dickens also describes a number of meals in the story, partly as a way of indicating characters or moods, and the account of food here can be compared with other descriptions later, as well as the account of Magwitch's eating in the first chapter.

Chapter 3

Summary

Pip takes the stolen goods to the stranger in the churchyard, but meets another escaped convict, who he thinks is Magwitch's 'young man', though he runs away at Pip's approach. Pip's stranger devours the 'wittles', but is startled to hear that another man with 'a badly bruised face' is nearby. Pip returns home as the stranger begins filing off his fetter.

Commentary

Pip's guilt is emphasised again but tempered by his feelings of humanity for the escaped convict, a quality which is to help him retain the reader's sympathy as he grows up and often behaves foolishly and snobbishly. The first complication of the plot begins to appear in this chapter as Pip wins the gratitude of the first convict, and learns that there is enmity between him and the second one, later identified as Compeyson.

Chapter 4
Summary

Pip returns to find Mrs Joe preparing Christmas dinner, his theft still undetected. Guests include Mr Wopsle, the church clerk, and Joe's Uncle Pumblechook, a corn-merchant. Uncle Pumblechook discovers with horror that the brandy he expected to drink has been replaced by tar-water, as Pip stole the brandy for the convict. Fearing discovery of his thefts when Mrs Joe prepares to serve the pork pie, Pip runs away, but is stopped by some soldiers at the door.

Commentary

Pip's guilt at robbing his sister is reinforced by the way Mrs Joe and her guests continually remind him of the trouble he has caused all his young life. Thus his sense of inferiority has been instilled in him since infancy, and even a Christmas dinner, normally an opportunity for celebration and love, is ruined. Pumblechook's pompous hypocrisy and Wopsle's theatrical ambitions, another kind of great expectations, begin to emerge, and we have another reference to hands, when Pumblechook reminds Pipe that he has been brought up 'by hand'.

Chapter 5

Summary
The soldiers are pursuing the two escaped convicts and need Joe to repair some handcuffs. Pip, Joe and Wopsle then accompany them out to the marshes, where they capture the convicts, though Pip's convict insists that he is handing over the other convict to the soldiers. Before being taken back to the prison-ship, Pip's convict exchanges glances with Pip and makes a statement confessing that he stole food and liquor from the blacksmith.

Commentary
The bleak landscape of the marshes and this frightening encounter with the convicts are both important elements in Pip's boyhood, and only his and Joe's pity for the convict offer relief in this scene. The quarrel between the convicts and the false confession of the theft are two pointers towards future developments in the novel.

Chapter 6

Summary
Exonerated by the convict's confession from the charge of theft, Pip has no scruples in concealing the truth from his sister, but regrets deceiving Joe who carries him home. Pumblechook describes how the theft must have taken place, and Mrs Joe puts Pip to bed.

Commentary
Though Pip does not mind concealing the truth about the robbery from his sister, he does feel guilty about deceiving Joe, whose confidence he fears losing. Thus Pip blames himself excessively for what he feels was cowardly and wicked behaviour. Yet another reference to 'hands' in this chapter links up with others throughout the book to give a kind of continuity, perhaps particularly important when the story was serialised, though the context of the hand-references varies from pleasant ones, as in a friendly handshake, to punitive ones.

Chapter 7

Summary

When old enough Pip is to be apprenticed to Joe, and until then he does odd jobs. Mr Wopsle's great-aunt teaches him reading and writing at evening school, and when Pip shows a letter he has written to Joe he discovers that Joe is almost illiterate, as his father was a drunken bully and prevented his education. Joe's father buillied his mother terribly, and this is why Joe tolerates his wife's aggressive manners to him and Pip rather than retaliating. Pip admires Joe for this. Mrs Joe announces that rich Miss Havisham wants a boy to go and play at her house, and sends Pip off to stay overnight with Pumblechook before visiting her.

Commentary

Joe's illiteracy and also his toleration of his wife's bullying ways are explained by his account of his own upbringing, and this makes him very appealing to Pip, though the reader may regret Joe's inability to offer Pip more protection. Mention of Miss Havisham introduces a new and major element into the narrative.

Chapter 8

Summary

Next day Pumblechook leads Pip to Miss Havisham's house, continually asking him questions to give him practice at mental arithmetic. A beautiful young girl, Estella, lets Pip into a darkened room where Miss Havisham greets him, wearing a faded yellow wedding-dress. She orders him to play cards with Estella, who treats him with contempt because of his coarse hands and thick boots. Miss Havisham tells him to return after six days, and orders him to be given some food. Pip cries at the way Estella humiliates him, and goes home very unhappy at the thought that he is 'a common labouring boy'.

Commentary

In this chapter Pip becomes aware of the way society regards the poor and uneducated through Estella's contempt for his coarse hands and boots, and his working-class language – he calls the third highest playing cards 'Jacks' and Estella calls them 'Knaves'. For the first time he feels shame for his supposed social inferiority, and wishes he had been brought up 'rather more genteelly'. Pip cannot help being attracted to Estella, however, despite the way she treats him, and his meeting with her is to develop into a long-lasting relationship.

In the portrait of Miss Havisham, Dickens introduces a deeply symbolical study of someone whom wealth has failed to make happy. Her name punningly suggests the phrase 'Having is a sham', as an indication of this, and the name of her house reiterates the idea, for Estella tells Pip that Miss Havisham's house is also known as Satis House, the word 'satis' being the Latin word for 'enough', meaning, she said, 'that whoever had this house could want for nothing else'. Miss Havisham has money and the house, but lacks love, however, for reasons which are to be made known later. (Dickens gives us a clue when he says that by laying her hands on her heart she reminds Pip of 'the young man' in Chapter 1, for Pip mistook Compeyson for that young man in the churchyard.) Miss Havisham has been so hurt by life that she has attempted to withdraw from the world and to freeze time, as the suspended wedding-breakfast and the stopped clocks indicate, but this is no answer to her problems, as the story will gradually reveal.

Chapter 9

Summary
When Pip returns home, he cannot bring himself to describe Miss Havisham as she really was, and makes up a story of her receiving him in a black velvet coach with four immense dogs, and of their playing flags together. Mrs Joe and Pumblechook are convinced that Miss Havisham will help Pip financially in some way. When Pip tells Joe that he has been lying, and about his shame at being thought common, Joe urges him to speak the truth and behave honestly.

Commentary
This chapter begins comically with Pip making up a hilarious imaginary account of his visit to Miss Havisham's because he feels that a truthful account would not be understood. When Pip confesses the truth to Joe, he feels guilty for telling lies, and Joe's honesty and simple dignity begin to emerge as a contrast to the behaviour of some of the wealthier, better-educated people in the novel. Pip continues to feel shame at being thought common by Estella, however. Mrs Joe and Uncle Pumblechook plant in Pip the idea that Miss Havisham may be going to help him in some way, and so help to sow the seed of Pip's great expectations later.

Chapter 10

Summary
Pip decides to try and make himself uncommon by improving his education, and asks Biddy, Mr Wopsle's great-aunt's school assistant and granddaughter, to help him. That evening when Pip calls for Joe at the inn, a stranger buys Joe and Wopsle a drink, and shows Pip he is stirring it with Joe's file. He gives Pip a new shilling, which Mrs Joe discovers is wrapped in two pound notes.

Commentary

Pip's determination to make himself acceptable to society in general and
Estella in particular leads him to try and improve his education, though
this does not prove very fruitful. The arrival of the secret-looking stranger
and his gift to Pip shows that the escaped convict (Magwitch) is grateful to
Pip for helping him, though Pip now feels ashamed of his contact with the
convict.

Chapter 11

Summary

On his next visit to Satis House, Pip meets Miss Havisham's sycophantic
relatives Cousin Raymond, Camilla and Sarah Pocket, and Georgiana, who
all criticise Matthew for not visiting Miss Havisham on her birthday. Miss
Havisham shows Pip her decayed wedding-cake and he plays cards with
Estella again. In the garden he fights and beats a strange, pale boy and
Estella lets him kiss her.

Commentary

Pip's acquaintance with Miss Havisham develops and he sees how other
people hope to inherit her money. He makes some progress in his relationship with Estella and meets two characters who are to become important
later, Jaggers and Herbert Pocket. The description of Miss Havisham's
loveless wedding-feast makes a vivid contrast to other meals in the novel,
such as Magwitch's in the churchyard and Pip's Christmas dinner. Some
readers criticise Dickens for depicting Jaggers both as the lawyer of Miss
Havisham and of Magwitch, a remarkable coincidence.

Chapter 12

Summary

Pip continues to visit Miss Havisham regularly, and she talks to him of his
ambitions, while encouraging his feelings for Estella. Pip tells no one of
this but Biddy, though Pumblechook and his sister continue to speculate
on what Miss Havisham will do for him. Miss Havisham invites Joe up to
Satis House with Pip's apprenticeship papers.

Commentary

Pip's ambitions to improve himself continue to grow, as well as his confused feelings about Estella. Thus his character is influenced by these
strange but glamorous surroundings, and perhaps encouraged by his sister's
and Pumblechook's worldly speculations. Joe is not sympathetic to Pip's
leaving the forge, however.

Chapter 13

Summary

Miss Havisham gives Joe twenty-five guineas to pay for Pip's apprenticeship, and Mrs Joe, Pumblechook and Wopsle celebrate with a dinner at the *Blue Boar*, though Pip does not enjoy it very much.

Commentary

Though he loves Joe, Pip is ashamed and embarrassed by his lack of social ease when speaking to Miss Havisham. He also feels trapped when apprenticed to become a blacksmith, for although the trade once looked attractive, Pip has developed new ideas since meeting Estella. Thus he does not enjoy the celebratory meal, particularly as he heard Miss Havisham tell Joe that he should not expect any further reward.

Chapter 14

Summary

Pip feels ashamed of home. Once he had admired it, but in the past year he has come to feel it coarse and common. Once he had hoped to work with Joe in the forge, but now he finds the thought depressing. Above all, he dreads being seen there by Estella.

Commentary

Though Pip (the narrator) is now middle-aged, he remembers the feelings of his youth vividly, especially the way he became ashamed of his home and work once he had met Estella and Miss Havisham. Yet even when he was growing ashamed, he was still able to admire Joe's good qualities, and this is one of the reasons Pip never quite loses the reader's sympathy.

Chapter 15

Summary

Pip completes his education and tries to pass his learning on to Joe, though without success. He continues to think of Estella and Miss Havisham, and asks Joe for a half-day holiday to visit them. Joe's workman Orlick is jealous of this and asks for a holiday too. When Mrs Joe objects, he insults her, and Joe gives him a thrashing. Pip is disappointed not to meet Estella at the House, but Miss Havisham tells him she is abroad being educated to become a lady. Returning home, Pip meets Wopsle who invites him to a play-reading at Pumblechook's. When Pip finally reaches home, he learns that his sister has been brutally attacked.

Commentary

Pip's fascination with Estella grows, and he begins to wish to become a gentleman. Two parallels to Pip's situation are also hinted at in this chapter.

Orlick claims parity of treatment with Pip over the half-day holiday, and it is clear that he is like (a violent) Pip in other ways, such as in his relationship with Mrs Joe. Wopsle's choice of a play, the tragedy of an ambitious apprentice who steals and murders for love, also mirrors Pip's feelings in an exaggerated way.

Chapter 16

Summary

Investigations fail to identify the attacker, and Mrs Joe is permanently crippled, losing the power of speech. A convict's leg-iron is found near the scene of the crime, and Pip believes that this belonged to his convict, and was used either by Orlick or the strange visitor. Biddy comes to help nurse Mrs Joe, and when she makes the shape of the letter 'T' Biddy realises that she is calling for Orlick who uses a hammer. Mrs Joe does not denounce Orlick as her attacker, however, but seems pleased to see him.

Commentary

Though literally innocent, Pip at first feels responsible for some part of the attack on his sister, perhaps because he had wished to strike her himself at times, and he even blames himself for having inadvertently provided the assault-weapon. Pip's boyhood feelings of guilt and inferiority are always important factors in understanding his later development. Mrs Joe's attitude towards Orlick is ambiguous, of course, not necessarily proving his innocence, but perhaps her desire to be friendly with him now.

Chapter 17

Summary

Pip settles into the routine of his apprenticeship, visiting Miss Havisham annually on her birthday. He becomes aware of Biddy's wholesome personality and intelligence, and one day tells her of Estella and his desire to become a gentleman. Though Biddy listens sympathetically, she warns him of the danger of his relationship with Estella, and Pip wishes he could love Biddy instead. She tells him of her dislike of Orlick, and Pip resolves to prevent him from courting her.

Commentary

Though Pip realises his dilemma, and is torn between love of Estella and ambition, and affection for Biddy and life on the marshes, this does not prevent his being insensitive to Biddy's feelings nor being a little hard on Orlick. He is in a thoroughly confused state, but retains a lingering hope that Miss Havisham will still make his fortune.

Chapter 18

Summary

In the fourth year of his apprenticeship, Mr Jaggers, a London lawyer, visits Pip and Joe to reveal that Pip has great expectations; he is to become the possessor of property, so he should leave the marshes and be brought up as a gentleman, for which money is already provided. Pip must not change his name or try to discover the identity of his benefactor. Though sorry to lose Pip, Joe agrees to release Pip from his apprenticeship without compensation. Joe and Biddy are pleased at Pip's good fortune, but Pip feels surprisingly gloomy that same evening.

Commentary

The plot intensifies its fairy-tale quality as Pip, the poor orphaned apprentice in love with a beautiful rich girl, discovers he has a fairy godmother (or godfather) to help him. His suspicion that the benefactor may be Miss Havisham is created partly by his memory of meeting Jaggers earlier and the suggestion of Matthew Pocket, Miss Havisham's relation, as his tutor. Jaggers contributes, in the talk at the inn, to the theme of justice and punishment, and it is important that the reader notices that his hands have 'the smell of scented soap' since this is a clue to the lawyer's character made clearer in Chapter 26. Though Pip is saddened by his awareness of what he will lose by becoming a gentleman, when he talks of new clothes he is already beginning to adopt the language and values of class-distinction.

Chapter 19

Summary

Pip prepares to leave and asks Biddy to help Joe improve himself while he is away. He buys a new suit from Trabb, the tailor, and is congratulated on his good fortune by Pumblechook. He bids Miss Havisham farewell, and spends a last sad evening with Joe and Biddy before taking the coach to London.

Commentary

Pip's growing snobbery is shown by his changing attitude towards Joe and the other townsfolk, whom he now begins to patronise, as well as by the way he enjoys the flattery of Trabb and the hitherto despised Pumblechook. Only Trabb's boy and Biddy seem to question his supposed superiority. In bidding farewell to Miss Havisham, Pip clearly reveals that he regards her as his 'fairy godmother'. This chapter ends the first stage of Pip's expectations, dealing with his boyhood in the marshes. The next stage of the novel will deal with Pip's manhood in London.

Chapter 20

Summary

Pip meets the lawyer Jaggers in London with his clerk, Wemmick. After Jaggers has dealt with a number of clients, he arranges for Pip to stay with Mr Pocket in Barnard's Inn.

Commentary

Pip finds London an ugly, dirty place, and the area he visits dominated by black church, filthy market and jail, not unlike William Blake's description of the city in his poem 'London'. The administration of the law is pervaded by money. Jaggers is willing to use a false witness, and though he is popular with his clients evidently treats them harshly.

Chapter 21

Summary

Wemmick escorts Pip to Barnard's Inn where Pip meets his room-mate, Mr Pocket, Junior, whom he recognises as the pale young gentleman he fought years earlier at Miss Havisham's.

Commentary

Wemmick is a dry, unforthcoming character, whom experience has evidently led to behave in a cautious, uncommunicative manner in his business affairs. Herbert Pocket is an open, ingenuous person, almost the opposite of Wemmick, though we note that he has to earn his own living, quite independent of patronage. Both characters have very important roles in the novel.

Chapter 22

Summary

The pale young gentleman introduces himself as Herbert Pocket, and his father is Miss Havisham's cousin. He promises to help Pip improve his manners and decides to call him 'Handel'. He reveals that Miss Havisham is the only daughter of a rich brewer, and was courted by a man with the connivance of her half-brother. Having obtained money from her, however, the bridegroom failed to turn up on the wedding-day, as a result of which Miss Havisham stopped all her clocks and laid Satis House waste. Herbert introduces Pip to his mother and father in Hammersmith.

Commentary

Though poor, Herbert and his father are gentle and honest, and make good foils to other 'gentlemen' in the novel. (Mr Pocket's definition of a gentleman is especially important.) Miss Havisham's story, as well as contributing to the unfolding of the plot, is also another comment on the dangers of wealth and false gentlemen.

Chapter 23

Summary
Mr and Mrs Pocket welcome Pip to their house where Pip is now to study with two other acquaintances, Bentley Drummle and Startop. Pip also meets Mrs Pocket's toady friend, Mrs Coiler. Mrs Pocket does not seem a very capable mother, though she has six children, and the household is dominated by the servants, one of whom gets drunk.

Commentary
Much of the comedy in this chapter is directed at Mrs Pocket for having aristocratic pretensions but being perfectly helpless and useless. The flattery of Mrs Coiler is also satirised. Drummle and Startop are introduced, two characters who are to become important later, and we also hear of Pip's resolve to improve his rowing, a decision which is to have important consequences in the plot later.

Chapter 24

Summary
Pip learns that he is to be educated not for a profession but to hold his own with other young men in prosperous circumstances. He decides to retain his bedroom in Barnard's Inn, and visits Jaggers for his approval. Jaggers gives him twenty pounds. Wemmick shows Pip the casts of two criminals and invites him to visit his home at Walworth. Pip sees Jaggers in action, dominating a law-court.

Commentary
The nature of Pip's education is revealed – he is to learn to be a gentleman – and this vocation is sharply contrasted with that of criminals who commit forgery or murder. Wemmick reveals the materialistic side of his character with his advice on property, and makes a reference to Australia which is deeply ironical in retrospect.

Chapter 25

Summary
Pip settles down to life as a rather extravagant leisured gentleman in London, deepening his acquaintance with Drummle and Startop, and becoming a close friend of Herbert's. Wemmick invites him home for an evening to his gothic cottage in Walworth with its drawbridge, moat, flagstaff and small gun. He introduces Pip to deaf father and shows him his legal souvenirs.

Commentary
Wemmick's cynical and materialistic behaviour in the office contrasts
sharply with the affectionate and creative personality he shows at home
for he tries to keep the business and private sides of his life quite separate.
The fact that his house is designed like a castle clearly suggests that it may
not be too secure. Pip's extravagance grows, and his interest in boating is
to have important consequences later.

Chapter 26

Summary
Jaggers invites Pip and his friends to his house in Soho and becomes
especially interested in Drummle, whom he calls 'the Spider', though he
persuades them all to reveal their worst features. When Drummle boasts of
the strength of his arms, Jaggers orders his housekeeper Molly to show her
amazingly powerful wrists. The evening ends with Pip quarrelling with
Drummle over money, but a month later Drummle's time with Mr Pocket
expires, and he goes home.

Commentary
Jaggers's power over people is displayed in this chapter while his unconscious unease with his work is also revealed by the way he is always washing his hands. The strength of Molly's hands links up with the same *motif*,
but her presence also prepares us for future revelations. Bentley Drummle's
brutal nature is also emphasised.

Chapter 27

Summary
Pip receives a letter from Biddy saying that Joe is coming to visit him in
London, and Pip wishes he could have paid him to stay away. Joe is clumsy
and uncomfortable with Pip and Herbert, and alternates between calling
the hero 'Pip' and 'Sir'. He brings a message from Miss Havisham to say
that Estella has come home and would be glad to see Pip.

Commentary
This chapter marks the change that is coming over Pip, as he feels ashamed
of Joe's intrusion into his 'gentlemanly' way of life. Joe recognises the
social gulf that is beginning to open up between them by the way he
addresses Pip and by his final words. The mention of the Blacking Warehouse is a private reference to Dickens' own childhood, and Joe's account
of Wopsle's London début comically mirrors another provincial's progress
in London.

Chapter 28

Summary

Pip travels to his home town the next day and finds there are also two convicts travelling to a prison-ship on the same coach. He recognises one as the man who gave him the two pound notes and hears him telling his companion of that very errand. Pip leaves the coach and makes his way to the *Blue Boar*, feeling a great dread. At the inn he discovers that Pumblechook is still claiming to be his benefactor.

Commentary

Pip's changing character is clearly brought out by his reluctance to stay with Joe on returning to the marshes. The coincidence of his re-meeting with the convict who delivered the pound notes earlier heightens the drama of the story and also demonstrates the way Pip is unable to escape from the consequences of his previous actions. Is Pip's fear based upon the (subconscious) recognition that Miss Havisham may not be his secret benefactor?

Chapter 29

Summary

Pip visits Miss Havisham, convinced that she intends to bring him and Estella together. He is shocked that Orlick has become her porter. At first he does not recognise Estella, who has grown into a beautiful young lady. Miss Havisham urges him to love her, though Estella tells him she has no heart or softness. Jaggers arrives and after dinner they play whist together. Pip wonders if Estella will ever love him as he loves her.

Commentary

Pip sees himself as the hero of a fairy tale and completely deceives himself about Miss Havisham's plans. His love for Estella grows, though she assures him that she lacks feeling. His admiration for her increases his feelings of shame for Joe and the past, but something about her appearance seems familiar (the hands?), though Pip is unable to say what.

Chapter 30

Summary

Pip tells Jaggers that Orlick is not suitable to be Miss Havisham's porter, and Jaggers promises to dismiss him. Pip is constantly teased by Trabb's boy when he walks down the High Street. On returning to London, he tells Herbert of his love for Estella, and Herbert tries in vain to persuade him to give her up. Then Herbert confesses that he is in love, too, with Clara, the daughter of an invalid.

Commentary

Pip's treatment of Orlick seems a little unkind, and Trabb's boy brilliantly and comically exposes Pip's false sense of social superiority to his local townsfolk. (Pip's letter to Trabb is pompous snobbery.) The conversation between Herbert and Pip reveals the precarious nature of Pip's expectations and enables Herbert to warn Pip that the way Miss Havisham has brought Estella up may cause Pip great unhappiness.

Chapter 31

Summary

Pip and Herbert go to the theatre to see Wopsle in *Hamlet*, but the actors are noisily barracked and Wopsle is laughed at. Backstage Pip and Herbert generously praise Wopsle, and he tells them that a rival actor has paid a member of the audience to barrack him.

Commentary

Wopsle thinks of himself as a gifted actor with a promising future, but is deceiving himself, as the hostile reception to his inept production of the play shows. Thus in a minor and humorous way Wopsle's ambitions and self-deception mirror Pip's in the novel's major plot.

Chapter 32

Summary

Estella writes to Pip telling him that she is coming to London and he goes to meet her. He meets Wemmick and accompanies him to Newgate Prison. He is struck by the way Wemmick knows the prisoners, including a man soon to be executed for counterfeiting coins. He also sees evidence of Jaggers' power everywhere.

Commentary

The description of the prisoners at the base of society contrasts sharply with that of the upper classes to whom Pip is now attaching himself. This prison visit reminds Pip of the various contacts he has had with convicts since his childhood, though he is not yet aware of how important they are. The appearance of Estella causes a brief moment of fear again.

Chapter 33

Summary

Pip meets Estella looking more beautiful than ever and takes her to tea. She tells him she is to live with a lady in Richmond who is to introduce her to people. Pip loves her and longs to be loved in return, but she behaves as if they are both puppets. He takes her to Richmond and thinks of consulting Mr Pocket.

Commentary

Though Pip does not fully realise it, Estella is now acting as Miss Havisham intended. She is beautiful and attracts Pip (and other men), but has been brought up to reject their love. Pip longs to be with her, but knows that it will never make him happy because of her lack of love. Estella's comments on the inmates of Newgate are, in view of her own parentage, deeply ironical.

Chapter 34

Summary

Pip notices that his great expectations are having a poor effect upon his behaviour, and he thinks he would have been happier if he had never met Miss Havisham. His lavish habits have led Herbert into extravagance, too. They join a club, the Finches of the Grove, and foolishly spend money in dissipation. Occasionally they sit down and make a list of their debts but do nothing about them. One day a letter arrives announcing Mrs Joe's death and inviting Pip to the funeral.

Commentary

Pip's wealth leads him to acquire the bad habits of false gentlemanliness, not to become a true gentleman, but he realises that he often behaves foolishly and is rarely very happy. This and his obvious concern for Herbert enable the reader to retain some sympathy for him.

Chapter 35

Summary

Pip is unable to believe that his sister is dead and wishes he could punish her attacker. Trabb organises an elaborate funeral, though Pumblechook mars it by his servile behaviour. Joe is pleased to see Pip, and Biddy describes how Mrs Joe tried to make her peace with him and Pip before she died. Pip promises to visit Joe more often and is angry when Biddy doubts his word.

Commentary

Mrs Joe's funeral provides the opportunity for Pip to be reconciled with Joe and Biddy, but Biddy doubts whether Pip will maintain the relationship, and annoys him by calling him 'Sir'. The elaborate funeral and Pumblechook's hypocrisy are satirised by Dickens, but in Mrs Joe's last words he suggests that she at least was capable of moral growth.

Chapter 36

Summary
Herbert and Pip get further into debt but on his twenty-first birthday Jaggers gives Pip five hundred pounds, telling him he will receive that sum annually until his benefactor appears. Though Jaggers refuses to divulge any further information Pip is convinced that Miss Havisham is his benefactor and intends him to marry Estella. Wemmick advises Pip not to use any of the money to help a friend.

Commentary
Pip's continued extravagance is emphasised and also his self-deception about Miss Havisham, though the reference to the tombstone and the two ghastly casts are ironic pointers to his real benefactor. That Pip is not entirely self-centred, however, is shown by his desire to use some of the money to help Herbert, and there is an amusing reference to the way Wemmick tries to separate his private from his professional life.

Chapter 37

Summary
Pip revisits Wemmick at his home and observes the affectionate way he looks after his deaf father, and his amusing courtship of Miss Skiffins. Wemmick also helps Pip to further Herbert's career by using some of Pip's money to buy Herbert a secret share in Clarriker's business.

Commentary
Wemmick's kindly behaviour at home is contrasted with his character in the office, and even his physical appearance changes. (The modest meal at home is one of love and friendship.) Pip's financial help for Herbert is the one good deed he knows that he has achieved. As this chapter ends an instalment of the serialised novel, Dickens points to a dramatic event which lies ahead.

Chapter 38

Summary
Pip sees Estella regularly at Mrs Brandley's house in Richmond, but his love for her is not really reciprocated and he is miserable. He accompanies her back to Satis House and witnesses a violent quarrel between Estella and Miss Havisham. Back in London, Bentley Drummle becomes friendly with Estella and she encourages the relationship, although she knows it makes Pip unhappy.

Commentary
This chapter, a whole episode in *All The Year Round*, concentrates on

Pip's relationship with Estella. The quarrel between Estella and Miss Havisham is written almost as a scene in a play, with heightened dialogue and 'stage-directions', and it is ironical for Miss Havisham to accuse Estella of being cold-hearted since that is what Miss Havisham has brought her up to be! (The description of the dark house, with its cobwebs and mice, is almost a symbol of Miss Havisham's diseased mind.) But though Pip recognises Estella's coldness and indeed is the recipient of her confidences, he still believes that she is intended for him once she has taken revenge on other men. Thus he goes on loving her, and resents her favour to Drummle. But Dickens is now preparing us for an amazing revelation, though events have been moving towards it from the very first chapter.

Chapter 39

Summary

Just after his twenty-third birthday, at 11 o'clock one stormy evening, Pip is visited by a stranger whom he recognises as the convict he helped on the marshes when he was a boy. The stranger reveals that he prospered after being transported overseas and used his money to make Pip a gentleman. Pip is shocked by the discovery that it is the convict, not Miss Havisham, who is his true benefactor, but puts the stranger up for the night to protect him from possible pursuers.

Commentary

The ironic discovery that Magwitch, not Miss Havisham, is Pip's benefactor has the force of the *Peripeteia*, or sudden change of fortune of a Greek tragedy, and this *narrative* discovery is paralleled by the beginnings of a *moral* discovery. Pip is shattered by the news, not only because of his realisation that he owes his fortune to a convict and has probably lost Estella, but also by his realisation that in becoming a 'gentleman' he has lost Joe.

With this dramatic and moral revelation, it is therefore very appropriate that Dickens ends the second stage of Pip's expectations. Though we may sympathise with Magwitch, it is clear that he intended to use Pip, as Miss Havisham uses Estella, to take revenge on society. Pip's resistance to phyical contact with Magwitch is very revealing.

Chapter 40

Summary

Pip falls over a man on the staircase of his chambers and is alarmed to discover that a stranger has been seen in the neighbourhood. He decides to pretend that Magwitch is his uncle Provis, and gets him new clothes and lodgings nearby. But Pip continues to fear and hate the ugly ex-convict with his coarse manners.

Commentary

The narrative now takes a new direction, as Pip begins to fear that Magwitch may be followed. He finds him physically repugnant, as we see from the way he loathes touching his hands. The new clothes are not much more successful in disguising the real Magwitch than Trabb's were in disguising Pip.

Chapter 41

Summary

Pip explains the presence of Magwitch to Herbert and says he cannot continue living on the ex-convict's money. Herbert points out that this will dash Magwitch's hopes and may lead to his recapture. Pip agrees that he must try to get Magwitch out of danger in England, and they ask him to tell his life story.

Commentary

Herbert seems to share Pip's aversion to Magwitch, but there is considerable irony in the fact that Pip resents help from Magwitch which he would have happily accepted from Miss Havisham. Pip does not wish to be grateful to a common criminal, but there is the beginning of some feeling towards him in the desire to protect Magwitch.

Chapter 42

Summary

Magwitch, abandoned as a child, had to beg and steal to keep himself alive. Through a partnership with Compeyson he moved into swindling and forgery, and saw how Compeyson's previous partner Arthur died in a delirious terror of a woman in white. When Compeyson and Magwitch were finally caught, Compeyson outwitted Magwitch at their trial, so Magwitch was the more severely punished, and vowed to take revenge. When Magwitch escaped from the Hulks, he helped recapture Compeyson. Herbert reveals to Pip that Arthur was Miss Havisham's half-brother, and that Compeyson was the man who deceived her.

Commentary

Magwitch's story moves Pip to pity for the first time, and also contains firm social comment on the unfair administration of law and justice between Magwitch and Compeyson. The latter is one of several 'false' gentlemen in the novel, and his part in the breakdown of Miss Havisham now becomes clear. Magwitch's Christian name Abel, the name of the innocent, murdered brother in the Old Testament, suggests that he is more innocent than first appeared, and his reticence over his wife, though perfectly natural, means that later revelations about her will have much more impact.

Chapter 43

Summary
Pip resolves to see Estella and Miss Havisham again before leaving England with Magwitch, but when he arrives in the marsh country he encounters Bentley Drummle at the *Blue Boar*. He and Pip exchange angry words before Drummle rides off to dine with a lady, and Pip thinks he sees Orlick at the inn.

Commentary
There is a beautiful irony in the way Pip resolves to keep his relationship with Estella a secret from Magwitch, and also in the way Pip now pretends he is visiting Joe when he is really going to Satis House. Orlick continues to be a uncomfortable presence.

Chapter 44

Summary
Pip accuses Miss Havisham of misleading him over the source of his wealth, but she says that he deceived himself and that Jagger's presence was a coincidence. Pip realises that Miss Havisham used him to make her relations jealous, and he asks her to continue his secret help of Herbert. He pours out a passionate declaration of his love to Estella, but she tells him that she has no feelings, and declares her intention of marrying Drummle. When Pip returns to London, he finds a note from Wemmick telling him not to go home.

Commentary
Pip's self-deception about his great expectations is now made quite clear. There are some signs of remorse in Miss Havisham's behaviour, however, and Pip's reformation continues as he persists in trying to help Herbert. Estella's reference to 'my mother by adoption' is another hint at future developments. Pip's declaration of love for Estella is deeply poignant, since he now believes that he has lost her for ever.

Chapter 45

Summary
After spending a restless night in a hotel in Covent Garden, Pip visits Wemmick who, without giving any names, reveals that he has learned that Magwitch's disappearance from Australia has been noticed, and that

Pip's chambers are being watched. (He also reveals that Compeyson is in London.) When he heard this, Wemmick visited Herbert, and helped him to transfer Magwitch to the house Clara lives in near the river Thames.

Commentary
The narrative now begins to concentrate on whether Pip can save Magwitch, and, as he tries to protect him, he becomes more concerned about the convict as a human being. The quality of Pip's previous lifestyle is reflected in Clara's poor opinion of him. Wemmick shows staunch human qualities away from the office.

Chapter 46

Summary
Pip finds Herbert at Clara's house near the Thames in Mill Pond Bank, and meets Clara there. Magwitch is safe, and Pip finds him softened in manner. They discuss Wemmick's plan for getting Magwitch abroad, and Pip acquires a boat with which he regularly practises rowing on the Thames.

Commentary
As the plan to get Magwitch safely out of the country gathers pace, Pip's attitude to him changes too. He notices that Magwitch has 'softened', and realises that Magwitch has risked his life for him. He becomes increasingly worried about Magwitch's safety. The account of Clara and her difficult father has some comic similarities to the Havisham-Estella relationship, but Pip envies the love between Clara and Herbert.

Chapter 47

Summary
Some weeks pass without any change, though Pip is pressed for money by his creditors and comes to believe that Estella is now married. One evening Pip goes to the theatre to see Wopsle act again, and after the performance Wopsle tells Pip he saw the convict whom Magwitch fought on the marshes sitting behind Pip in the theatre. Compeyson has vanished, however.

Commentary
Wopsle's theatrical career has declined as Pip's expectations of becoming a rich gentleman have declined too, though in Pip's case it is because he has decided to return Magwitch's money. Wopsle's recognition of Compeyson after so many years might seem unconvincing except that he remembers their first encounter in graphic detail.

Chapter 48

Summary
A week later Pip is invited to dinner by Jaggers, and learns that Miss Havisham wants to see him. Jaggers implies that Drummle has married Estella, and that there may be conflict between them. Pip notices Molly's hands again and becomes convinced that she is Estella's mother. On the way home afterwards Wemmick tells Pip that Molly was tried for murder but successfully defended by Jaggers. She was also suspected of murdering her three-year-old daughter.

Commentary
Wemmick's business behaviour is strongly contrasted with his private character again. Jaggers's reference to Estella's marriage points to its possible failure in the future. But the major feature of this chapter is the discovery of the identity of Estella's mother, another example of the ways Dickens uses hand-references in the novel. There is massive irony in Pip's feeling unworthy of Estella earlier, now that her real social origins are known.

Chapter 49

Summary
Pip revisits Miss Havisham and finds her changed. She agrees to give him £900 to help Herbert, and asks Pip's forgiveness for the wrong she has done him in the past. She describes how she adopted Estella as a young girl with Jagger's help, and regrets the way she brought her up. Just as Pip is leaving, he sees Miss Havisham enveloped in flames, and, though he rushes to help her, she is seriously hurt. Pip is astonished to see that his own hands are burnt, too.

Commentary
The main purpose of this chapter is to reveal how Miss Havisham has realised the folly and cruelty of her training of Estella, and how she tries to make amends by asking forgiveness and helping Herbert. (The death of the old Miss Havisham is symbolised by Pip's fancy of her hanging herself and by the fire.) Pip's growing compassion is illustrated by the way he can now pity and forgive her, but he is not to escape unharmed from the experience and his burnt hands are the symbolical as well as physical signs of the damage he has suffered.

Chapter 50

Summary
Pip returns to London where he is well nursed by Herbert. Herbert has

found Magwitch more sympathetic and heard from him the story of how his woman was acquitted of a murder charge and of how their child disappeared. Pip tells Herbert that he believes Magwitch is Estella's father.

Commentary
Dickens is essentially a *popular* novelist, and at the narrative level, having revealed the source of Pip's unexpected wealth, is now proceeding to unravel the mystery of the identity of Estella's parents, while Magwitch's dangerous predicament also continues to provide narrative suspense. The coincidence of Pip's meeting Estella's father so many years ago, and of meeting and loving Estella at Satis House shortly afterwards, though it would probably have been defended by Dickens as literally possible, can also be seen as appropriate for the fairy-tale form Dickens has adopted to articulate his moral and social themes.

Chapter 51

Summary
Pip visits Jaggers, and arranges for Miss Havisham's money to be used for Herbert. He then pursues the question of Estella's parentage, and Jaggers discusses the case of a woman being prosecuted and her child being put in the care of an eccentric rich lady. He argues that no good will be done by revealing the child's origins.

Commentary
Apart from confirmation of Estella's parentage, this chapter is interesting for its revelation that Jaggers has kindly feelings which he normally tries to conceal in the office, and that he is astonished to discover the same thing about Wemmick! That their cold business manner is deliberately adopted is seen from the unsympathetic way they both turn on Mike at the end of the chapter. It is not a comfortable strategy, however, and Wemmick's advice about 'portable property' strikes a disconcerting note.

Chapter 52

Summary
Pip arranges for Miss Havisham's money to help Herbert's business, and learns that he will take charge of the Eastern office. Wemmick advises Pip to get Magwitch out of the country and they arrange for Startop to help them row down the Thames past Gravesend, so Pip and Magwitch can catch a steamer to Hamburg. An anonymous note summons Pip to a meeting on the marshes that evening, and Pip takes a walk around his old town.

Commentary

Pip's moral reform continues not only as he tries to help Herbert, but in
the feeling of shame he has for his treatment of Joe. Pumblechook evidently complains of Pip's ingratitude to him, but Pip realises that he owes
more gratitude towards Joe, who never complains of his treatment.

Chapter 53

Summary

Pip makes his way to his mysterious assignation on the marshes, and is
there attacked and bound by Orlick who plans to kill him. Led by Trabb's
boy, however, Herbert and Startop come to Pip's rescue (Herbert discovered
the anonymous note which Pip dropped in their chambers and, alarmed
by its tone, hastened down to the marshes with Startop. Trabb's boy
guided them to the sluice-house.) Though Pip's arm is badly injured, they
return to London and propose to smuggle Magwitch down river.

Commentary

This dramatic chapter obviously adds to the narrative excitement of the
novel, but raises some interesting questions about Orlick. Though he is
a villain, his accusations contain some truth, and his statement that Pip
killed Mrs Joe suggests that Orlick did what Pip himself would have liked
to have done. (Is Orlick Pip's other self?) Pip has been unfair to Trabb's
boy earlier in the novel, and it is interesting that Pip is now able to recognise his merits and to behave generously towards him.

Chapter 54

Summary

Herbert and Startop row down river while Pip steers. They pick up Magwitch
at Mill Pond Stairs and spend the night at a public house below Gravesend.
When they row out to join the Hamburg steamer next day, however, a
four-oared galley pulls alongside and the steersman tries to arrest Magwitch.
The Hamburg steamer bears down on both of the smaller boats; Magwitch
exposes one of his pursuers in the galley as Compeyson, and, in the ensuing
confusion and shouting, both men go overboard, Pip's boat sinks, and
Compeyson is drowned. The officer in charge takes Magwitch back to
London.

Commentary

Dickens handles the narrative superbly throughout this chapter by a
combination of convincing small details, such as the references to other
river traffic, and a growing sense of menace created, for example, by the
conversation in the public house about seeing men from the Custom
House. Pip's feeling for Magwitch, once so hostile, has gradually turned

to love, as his willingness to hold hands shows. It is particularly moving that now, when Magwitch suggests to Pip that contact between them will damage Pip's reputation as a gentleman, it is Pip who asserts that he will never leave Magwitch's side.

Chapter 55

Summary

Magwitch is committed for trial. Herbert tells Pip that business will take him abroad and invites him to join the firm, but Pip feels that he must stay with Magwitch for the present. Wemmick discloses that Compeyson had been on Magwitch's trial for some time, and he apologises for letting Compeyson outwit him. Wemmick tells Pip that he is going to take a holiday, and invites Pip to join him on a holiday walk. When Pip keeps the appointment, he is surprised to discover that the walk leads to a church where Wemmick marries Miss Skiffins!

Commentary

In his loyalty to Magwitch, Pip is willing to abandon all his financial expectations now, much to Jagger's disjust. Wemmick's dual combination of prudence and affection is even more marked, and his wedding, which begins as a walk with a fishing-rod, and is accompanied by a series of apparently accidental discoveries of a church, a pair of gloves, Miss Skiffins, and finally a wedding-ring, is one of the best comic episodes in the novel.

Chapter 56

Summary

Magwitch lies in prison very ill and is regularly visited by Pip, who, even at his trial, continues to hold Magwitch's hand. The Judge singles Magwitch out for particular reproof and sentences him to death. Pip continues to visit him in prison while he is awaiting execution, and, just before Magwitch dies, reveals that his daughter has grown up to become a beautiful woman, and that he, Pip, loves her.

Commentary

Pip's love for the dying criminal whom he had once hated is beautifully revealed by the way they now hold hands and communicate physically, where once Pip could not bear the touch of Magwitch. Though Dickens does not blame the officers of the law, his account of the law itself suggests that it falls cruelly short of real justice.

Chapter 57

Summary

Pip falls ill and is unable to pay his debts, but Joe nurses him back to health. He reveals that Miss Havisham has died, leaving Matthew Pocket £4 000 and her other relations small legacies, and that Orlick has been arrested for robbing Pumblechook. Pip decides to travel down to the marshes to beg Joe's forgiveness, and to propose to Biddy, if she will have him.

Commentary

Pip's moral reformation is almost complete now and he hopes to cement his recovery by returning to his old home on the marshes, to marry Biddy, and perhaps to return to work in the forge with Joe. But Joe reveals that there is still some gap between them by calling him 'Sir' as Pip recovers his health. In proposing to marry Biddy, Pip forgets that she, too, is a person in her own right, with her own desires and feelings. Among the items of local news that Joe brings to Pip is the important information that Miss Havisham completed her transformation before she died, and even the account of Orlick is not unsympathetic.

Chapter 58

Summary

When Pip reaches the marshes he discovers that news of his financial plight has preceded him. Pumblechook meets him and attributes his fall to ingratitude. Pip finds Biddy and Joe celebrating their marriage, and so leaves after begging their forgiveness. He joins Herbert's business abroad and after many years becomes a partner, too.

Commentary

The main feature of this chapter is Pip's complete reconciliation with Biddy and Joe, and his frank recognition of his bad behaviour in the past. He is able to treat Pumblechook as a complete imposter now, and coolly observes the behaviour of other hypocrites. But Pip is not able to put the clock back to his own childhood, and has to learn to live in the world as it is now. Though unmarried, he achieved a modest degree of happiness as the years pass.

Chapter 59

Summary

Eleven years later Pip returns home from abroad to find Joe and Biddy with two young children, their boy the image of the young Pip. Pip tells Biddy that he has never forgotten Estella, and that evening when he re-visits Satis House he finds no house there, but Estella in the garden. She is much changed, for her husband gave her an unhappy time until he died two years earlier. They leave the garden together hand in hand.

Commentary

Estella has been softened by her unhappy experiences, and is now able to understand and love Pip more. Pip, too, has changed and becomes wiser as a result of his experiences. They are thus now able to establish a new and better relationship and, as they leave the garden together, Dickens's language echoes John Milton's description of Adam and Eve making a new start after their Fall in *Paradise Lost*. There is a muted and even ambiguous quality about this *revised* ending of the novel, however, far from the conventional picture of orange blossom and wedding-bells it is taken to be, for the reader cannot be quite certain as to what the new relationship between Pip and Estella will be.

3 THEMES AND ISSUES

Great Expectations is a novel which, in telling the story of a young boy and his growth to manhood, takes as its major theme the effects of up-bringing and environment upon character, the ways they can almost dehumanise personality, and the ways in which sympathy and love can restore humanity.

Though the novel is a beautifully integrated work, in which no single part can be properly discussed without reference to the other parts, it may be helpful to think of the book from three different perspectives, as a *fictional narrative*, as *an account of moral and psychological development*, and as *a novel about different aspects of society*.

3.1 NARRATIVE

As a narrative *Great Expectations* abounds in exciting events, mysteries, unexpected revelations, extraordinary characters, violence, love stories, humour, and a modestly happy ending. Dickens was a novelist who took his responsibilities as a popular story-teller seriously, and knew that in order to retain his reader's interest from one week's issue of *All the Year Round* to the next he had to give value for money.

Thus the novel begins at once with the dramatic encounter between the young Pip and the runaway convict in the churchyard on Christmas Eve. Later events add to this powerful, brooding atmosphere in the book, and Joe's fight with Orlick, the brutal attack on Mrs Joe, the dramatic return of Magwitch to London, Pip's fight with Orlick, and the desperate attempt to row Magwitch to safety down the river, all help to maintain this air of the unexpected and the violent.

One of the most important ways Dickens holds the reader's attention throughout the story is by his use of mysteries. He is particularly skilful at revealing problems in the plot and keeping the reader (and characters in the novel) guessing as to their solution. Then, as one mystery is solved, Dickens proceeds to lead us on to wonder about the solution of a new problem. The greatest mystery in *Great Expectations* is, of course, the mystery of who left Pip the money to become a gentleman. This problem is not solved until the final third of the novel, but Dickens also exploits the plot to raise other mysteries. Why does Miss Havisham behave in the way she does? Who attacked Mrs Joe? Who is shadowing Pip in London? Will Pip and Herbert succeed in saving Magwitch? Who are Estella's real parents? By raising these kinds of questions Dickens continues to hold the reader's interest in something like the way a writer of detective stories does.

Another way Dickens uses to keep the reader's interest is by telling a love story about the fluctuating relationship between a man and a woman, and though *Great Expectations* concentrates on the story of Pip and Estella, and we are never quite sure whether Pip will marry Estella or not, it is important to remember that Pip's is not the only love story in the novel, for we also hear of Joe and Biddy, as well as Herbert and Clara, and of Mr Wemmick and Miss Skiffins.

Finally, Dickens's narrative art is enriched, not only by his use of dramatic encounters and mysteries and love stories, but also by his genius for comedy and the creation of memorable characters. The presence of such extraordinary figures as Uncle Pumblechook, Miss Havisham, Wemmick and Mr Wopsle, gives the story a marvellous energy. Few readers are likely to forget such scenes as Pip's first visit to Satis House, or Uncle Pumblechook's prolonged congratulations of Pip when he first learns of his expectations, or Mr Wemmick's treatment of his Aged Parent at Walworth! From its brilliant beginning to its poignant close, *Great Expectations* has few equals among Dickens's novels for its narrative strength and richness.

3.2 MORAL AND PSYCHOLOGICAL DEVELOPMENT

Though *Great Expectations* obviously possesses a very strong narrative appeal, as a superb example of powerful and popular elements, it is also clear that in focusing upon certain events in Pip's life from the time when he was a small boy on the marshes to his becoming a middle-aged business-man, Dickens is using the story to paint a powerful picture of Pip's moral and psychological development. We see how his origins and environment help to shape his personality and give him views and attitudes which gradually lead him into snobbish and unfeeling ways, but how, from the combination of his personality and later experiences, he finds some kind of integrity and harmony again.

The first important aspect of Pip's early life is the fact that he is an orphan. His parents and all his brothers lie buried in the local churchyard, and his speculations about their tombstone immediately tells us something about Pip's sensitive and imaginative nature. He has first-hand knowledge that life is short and brutal, and the harsh landscape with its gibbet adds to that impression.

He is, it is true, brought up by his older sister, but she is hard and unfeeling, constantly punishing him for apparently trivial offences, and above all constantly making him feel guilty, not only for committing these offences but for being dependent on her, and not feeling sufficient gratitude towards her for keeping him alive. This sense of guilt is reinforced by Pumblechook's bullying behaviour and dominating influence on the household. It is no wonder that the small boy feels so lost and inadequate, the abbreviation of his Christian name perhaps suggesting the way his identity is threatened.

The encounter with Magwitch, the escaped convict, in the churchyard, accentuates Pip's feelings of guilt, since he is so terrfied of the convict's threats that he is forced to steal. By this action he believes that he too has become a criminal, and his sense of guilt is increased by the fact that he does not feel able to tell Joe what he has done. Such early experiences help to explain a lot of Pip's later development.

The visits to Miss Havisham and Satis House reinforces Pip's feeling of inadequacy, for they add to his guilt a sense of social inferiority. Though Dickens is able to show his readers the limitations of Miss Havisham's world, the deprived Pip finds it a world of romance and beauty, but one from which he may be excluded because of his coarse working-class appearance and manners. To Estella he is only 'a common labouring boy' (Chapter 8).

Other experiences resulting from the visits to Satis House further heighten Pip's feeling of guilt, such as when, unable to describe Miss Havisham's truly extraordinary appearance, he makes up the story of the black velvet coach and four dogs, and Joe reproves him, all the more painfully by his gentleness, for telling lies. The outcome of the fight with the pale young gentleman also worries Pip who thinks he may be thrown into the county jail for his violence!

These feelings of guilt and shame continue to dominate Pip's youth, leading to his ambition to become a gentleman as a way of winning Estella and achieving some kind of esteem. He gradually becomes more aware and ashamed of Joe's limitations, especially his illiteracy and his lack of social ease when talking to Miss Havisham, and whereas once he had looked forward to working with Joe in the forge, he comes to find that prospect depressing, particularly the thought that Estella might see him there. At the same time he cannot help feeling guilty about the violent attack on his sister, not only because the assault-weapon was his convict's leg-iron but because he had never told the truth about that to Joe. (He may also have nursed an unconscious wish to hurt his sister, as Orlick claims later.)

Pip's wishes to escape from this world of guilt and shame, of deprivation and inadequacy, and to do so by becoming a gentleman, are apparently fulfilled by the news of his great expectations brought by Mr Jaggers in Chapter 18. Pip gradually adopts the worldly values of gentlemanliness, expensive clothes, servants, membership of a club, and more formal manners, and gradually begins to disregard such qualities as good-heartedness, steady industry and gratitude.

We can see these changes beginning to appear in Pip's new attitude towards the formerly-despised Pumblechook and Trabb, the local tailor, almost immediately he comes into his good fortune. Pip's letter to Trabb in Chapter 30 is an example of his pompous snobbery. The fullest register of Pip's moral shabbiness is revealed, not only by the extravagance and dissipation of his club-life in London, but by his embarrassment and shame at meeting Joe, wishing that he would not come to London, and avoiding him when returning to the marsh country to see Estella.

Pip never entirely loses his decent feelings, of course; he *is* frequently embarrassed by his treatment of Joe and by Biddy's reproaches. Another sign of his goodness is the way he tries to help Herbert, whose virtues he gradually comes to appreciate, with some of his newly-acquired wealth – 'the only good thing I had done', he says in Chapter 52.

But Pip's feeling of guilt and shame are reawakened by the return of Magwitch in Chapter 39, and his initial response to the ex-convict's reappearance is aversion and repugnance. Magwitch is a frightening criminal who reminds Pip of his own guilt; he has tried to manipulate Pip, and his patronage probably means that Pip has lost Estella. But in Chapter 42 Pip begins to feel pity for Magwitch for the first time, when he hears the story of his hard life, and he becomes deeply involved when he plans to save him from possible execution. He realises that Magwitch has risked his life to see him again.

Similarly, though Pip reproached Miss Havisham for misleading him over the identity of his benefactor, and for her training of Estella, he is able to forgive her and help rescue her, when he recognises her lonely unhappiness in Chapter 49.

Having almost been killed in the fire at Satis House, and then in the subsequent encounter with Orlick, Pip is virtually reborn when he returns to London and his plan to take Magwitch to safety down the river:

> As I looked along the clustered roofs, with Church towers and spires shooting into the unusually clear air, the sun rose up, and a veil seemed to be drawn from the river, and millions of sparkles

burst out upon the waters. *From me too, a veil seemed to be drawn, and I felt strong and well.* [My italics] (Chapter 53)

Nothing is more indicative of Pip's moral growth than the way he stands by Magwitch at the trial, literally and symbolically, now proud to hold the hand of the man he once abhorred to touch. His illness and recovery from it are further signs of the moral regeneration, which gives him the maturity to retrace his steps to the marsh country he was so glad to escape from earlier and, despite the humiliation of Pumblechook, beg forgiveness of Joe and Biddy.

It is not possible for Pip to return completely to his way of life before he had great expectations, however, as he had hoped when in Chapter 57 he thought he might marry Biddy and work again in the forge with Joe. Biddy is married to Joe, and Pip has to live in the world as it is now. He does this by accepting the situation gracefully, paying his debts, and then going abroad to work as a clerk, and live modestly with Herbert and Clara.

The reunion with Estella in the last chapter is the final sign that Pip is freed from the feelings of guilt and shame which haunted his youth, and from the social ambitions that were the result of those feelings. The Estella he meets now has lost much of her beauty and her wealth, but has learned from her experiences too, so they accept each other in honesty for what they are.

This change in Estella reminds us that, though Pip is the main protagonist through whom Dickens discusses his theme of upbringing, dehumanisation and love, there are other characters in the novel who also illustrate aspects of his great theme, including not only Estella and Miss Havisham, but even Mrs Joe and Magwitch to some extent. All have been hardened and coarsened by harsh experiences in their lives, and all show signs of growing into more humane feelings by the end.

3.3 ASPECTS OF SOCIETY

Great Expectations is more than a study of personal and psychological development, however, for in telling Pip's story Dickens inevitably has a good deal to say about the society in which Pip lives, about its cruelties and the different ways people try to cope with them, and Dickens also has much to say about such themes as crime, justice and the law, about the nature of gentlemanly virtues, and about the problems created by confusion between appearance and reality, and by self-deception.

Viewed as a picture of society, *Great Expectations* depicts an extremely harsh world. Pip himself is the clearest example of this, of course, orphaned, brought up by an unfeeling sister, and manipulated both by Miss Havisham and by Magwitch, mainly in retaliation for the cruelties life has inflicted on them. Compeyson's cruel trickery of Miss Havisham, in which he is actually aided by her half-brother, triggers off the whole plot, and Compeyson later exploits Magwitch, thus generating the violent feud between them. Magwitch's own life has always been a harsh one, his crime caused by the poverty he suffered from boyhood, and the story of his wife Molly, herself tried for murder, darkens that impression further. Orlick's assaults on Mrs Joe, and then upon Pip, Bentley Drummle's treatment of Estella, the unfairness of the legal system, all build up a picture of a brutal, exploitative and unjust society. Life in London, with its dirt and corruption and prisons, as depicted in Chapter 20 is no better than Pip's bleak life on the marshes, with the bullying and the gibbet and the Hulks. It is no wonder that so many people long to escape.

The commonest way of trying to survive in such a world is through wealth and social position. This is the path Pip follows in the first two-thirds of the book, and he is not alone in this. Miss Havisham's relations Sarah, Georgiana and Camilla Pocket, have the same kind of ambition, and so in their different ways do Mrs Joe and Pumblechook, Magwitch and Wopsle. Though Pip is the prime example of great expectations in the novel, he is not the only one.

Miss Havisham has learned that the possession of money is no guarantee of avoiding cruelty and unhappiness, however, and her way of dealing with society's harshness is to withdraw from life as much as possible, and to live in isolation. She attempts to freeze time at the moment when she was jilted and to prevent any intrusions from the outside world, hoping to take her revenge for the wrongs inflicted on her by using Estella to break men's hearts. In the ironical name of her house and its ugly, decaying interior as well as in her belated reform, Dickens shows the futility of this kind of response to life's cruelties.

Wemmick illustrates yet another kind of response, by trying to keep his private life at home quite separate from his business life. At work in the City, he treats clients harshly and displays a cynical contempt for everything except property; but at home in Walworth he is a loyal friend, who looks after his aged father with great tenderness, and is willing to go to a good deal of trouble on Pip's behalf. The precarious nature of his home, appropriately named the Castle, suggests, however, that Dickens does not consider that this kind of approach to life is likely to be very effective in the long run. Jaggers has many similarities to Wemmick, the main difference being that his veneer of business-toughness is much deeper, and the kind heart it conceals is only revealed towards the end of the novel. His incessant hand-washing surely reveals his deep dissatisfaction with the way he earns his money.

In Dickens's view the only way to live in the harsh world Victorian England became, without cutting oneself off from all society in an atrophying isolationism, was neither to try to separate one's private life from one's business life nor to rely on expectations of unearned wealth, but rather to be content to work within that society as decently as possible, and with a mature appreciation both on one's fellowmen and of oneself.

Discussion of Wemmick and Jaggers, however, inevitable draws attention to the importance of crime and justice, law and punishment in the novel, as plot elements and as major themes. The opening chapter describes an escaped convict forcing a young boy to steal; another escaped convict appears in Chapter 3; and both are soon sent back to a prison-ship. Jaggers and Wemmick, both connected with the law, play major parts in Pip's story, which also includes his visiting Newgate Prison in Chapter 32 and a prison infirmary in Chapter 56. Orlick commits two criminal assaults and a burglary, and Molly's history includes being tried for murder at the Old Bailey.

Indeed it can be argued that crime, in the person of Compeyson, is the prime mover of the plot, for, after robbing her of a good deal of her fortune, he jilted Miss Havisham and thus turned her against men, while in corrupting Magwitch he put in train the events which led to Pip's expectations. Most important of all, however, is the fact that when Compeyson and Magwitch were tried for their crimes, the impartiality of the judicial system is shown to be a myth, for judge and jury alike are swayed by prejudice in favour of Compeyson's appearance as a gentleman, and he receives a lighter sentence.

In the picture of the legal system in Chapter 20, in the numerous accounts of Jaggers and Wemmick and their clients, and above all in the great trial scene in Chapter 56, Dickens is clearly saying that real justice is very hard to find, and that there is very little correlation between justice and punishment in English society because of poverty and the class system. Magwitch, unlike Compeyson, never had a chance, and, though he is not completely innocent, Pip is absolutely justified in asking for a mercy for him which the legal system is unable even to recognise, let alone offer.

Compeyson, of course, is better treated by the law because, although he is a villain, his public-school education and smooth talk, his black clothes and white pocket-handkerchief give him the appearance of a gentleman, when compared with the ragged Magwitch. The nature of being a gentleman forms another theme of *Great Expectations*, for there are several aspirants to that rank in the novel, including not only Compeyson, but Startop, Bentley Drummle and Pip herself. Pip's notions of a gentleman are very much based upon forms of dress, speech and expensive habits, however, and it is a painful part of his education that he only gradually comes to appreciate the truth of Mr Pocket's principle that: 'No man who was not a true gentleman at heart, ever was since the world began, a true gentleman in manner' (Chapter 22), Bentley Drummle has the formal requisites to be a gentleman and Joe Gargery lacks them, but Dickens does not leave us in any doubt as to who is the better man.

Discussion of gentlemen and their appearance connects with another theme in the novel, Dickens' treatment of appearance, reality and self-deception. The major example of self-deception is, of course, the way Pip believes that the source of his expectations is Miss Havisham, and that she is paying for him to become a gentleman so that he can marry Estella, when his real benefactor is Magwitch. (Pip's expectations are paralleled in a minor way by Wopsle's ambition to become a famous actor, another unfulfilled ambition.)

Pip's misunderstanding and self-deception about the source of his wealth, despite several clues to the contrary, are paralledled by his moral self-deception about what he thinks will bring him happiness, the life of a wealthy gentleman, again despite several indications to the contrary. It is only at the end of the novel that Pip realises he has been following false values imposed upon him by other people, and it is no coincidence that this moral discovery comes just after Pip's dramatic discovery of the real identity of his secret benefactor.

There are many examples of people not being what they seem in the novel. Wemmick and Jaggers both seem cold and unfeeling at first, but have kindlier impulses beneath their businesslike exteriors, while Magwitch is perhaps the supreme example of the falsity of an unpleasant appearance, for though ugly and uncouth, he proves to be a man of lovable personality.

Among characters who hypocritically effect an appearance of concern but are basically selfish, Uncle Pumblechook is outstanding. Mr and Mrs Camilla Pocket and Georgiana fawn upon Pip in his prosperity, of course, as does Mr Trabb, the local tailor, and Mrs Coiler, the Pockets' toady neighbour. The hypocrisy of these characters is based upon wealth and snobbery, and it is to Pip's discredit that he too develops similar weaknesses for a time, confusing Joe's lack of elegance with a lack of good-heartedness.

The theme of appearance and reality, in other words, cannot be separated from the other issues Dickens is dealing with in the novel such as the nature of a true gentleman or the problems of justice and punishment. The picture *Great Expectations* offers us of nineteenth-century society has important bearings on all these themes as well as upon Dickens's passionate interest in the effects of such a society upon the individual's moral and psychological development. The whole work is beautifully integrated.

4 TECHNICAL FEATURES

4.1 PLOT AND STRUCTURE

On the surface *Great Expectations* belongs to that class of nineteenth-century novels, sometimes called education or development novels in English or *bildungsroman* in German, which tell the story of a young man of talent but humble origins, who travels from the countryside to a large city where he gradually climbs the social ladder, often winning wealth and wisdom in the process, though losing something of his early innocence. Stendhal's *Le Rouge et le Noir* and Honoré de Balzac's *Le Père Goriot* are two French examples of this form, while Henry Fielding's eighteenth-century novel *Tom Jones* has some of the same characteristics in its story of how the illegitimate young hero travels from Somerset to London, discovers the identity of his parents, and marries the lovely heroine.

Like such contemporary novelists as George Eliot and Charlotte Brontë Dickens used recent history rather than the remote past to give realism to his story. The reference of Old London Bridge in Chapter 46 helps the reader to date the main action of the later stage of Pip's expectations as about the year 1823 because the new London Bridge was not begun until 1824, and since we know that Pip was aged about 23 then, we can see that the novel actually begins about 1807 when Pip was 'about 7'. Though Dickens (and Pip) are writing about the main events in the story years after they happened, the sense of the period 1807–23, during which the main events took place, is established with great care. The accounts of journeys by stage coach, the description of hulks on the Thames being used as prison-ships, and even the reference to tar-water being used as a medicine all help to build up a realistic picture of the period.

Beneath this surface of nineteenth-century realism, however, the plot of *Great Expectations* clearly employs many of the elements of traditional folk and fairy tales in its structure, as even the briefest summary indicates. One Christmas Eve a poor orphan-boy meets a terrifying stranger in a churchyard and has his first encounter with violence in the form of Magwitch (The name itself suggests a wicked magician.) A fairy godmother, Miss Havisham, befriends the boy, introducing him to a beautiful princess, Estella, and encouring his ambitions, so that the young apprentice, like Dick Whittington, longs to become rich and marry her. After a journey to London and many adventures, including a fight almost to the death with another adversary, Orlick, the young hero finally comes to manhood and security.

Such a story, we can see, clearly contains ingredients found in many folk and fairy tales, of which *Dick Whittington* and *The Beauty and The Beast* are the most obvious. What is interesting about Dicken's use of such familiar *motifs* from folk tales, however, is the way he varies and indeed inverts the expected patterns. Traditionally the hero ends his adventures rich and successful as the ruler of a large kingdom or a Lord Mayor at least, but Pip finishes up only a moderately well-paid, middle-aged business-man, with his marriage to the princess by no means assured. Similarly the Ugly Monster Pip meets in the churchyard proves to be a lovable character, while Pip's apparent benefactress and godmother turns out to be more like a wicked witch for most of the story. Dickens relies on the elements of the folk tale for the plot of *Great Expectations*, in other words, but deepens it, not only by means of a surface realism but by making many subtle and ironical variations of the traditional structure.

The structure of *Great Expectations* also has some of the characteristics of the narrative pattern of many Greek tragedies. These often told the story of a man who prospered and achieved great success, perhaps becoming a king or a famous hero. In the course of his career, however, the hero commits the sin of *hubris* or pride, and in trying to solve some problem or right some wrong in his kingdom, the hero makes a vital, perhaps even shocking, discovery that leads to his downfall as a kind of divine punishment for his pride. (The story of Oedipus, as told in Sophocle' play *Oedipus the King* is the supreme example of this kind of story.) In *Great Expectations* Pip pursues his ambition to become a gentleman, and behaves arrogantly to Joe and Biddy in the process. In Chapter 39, however, Pip discovers that his real benefactor is Magwitch, not Miss Havisham as he had long believed, and this discovery leads to a dramatic change, a reversal in fact, of Pip's material fortunes. There is an irony about Pip's material fall which is very similar to that found in many Greek plays.

Dickens's use of the kind of structure which depends on the presence of traditional narrative elements has several positive advantages. It reassures the reader psychologically that he or she is on familiar ground, even when the plot seems complicated and the characters confusing, an important factor when a novel was being serialised weekly or monthly, and could therefore only be read in short episodes. More importantly, however,

Dicken's adoption of a familiar story-line anabled him not only to reach a wider audience but his skill at varying it, for example by showing how the traditional beast-figure can be lovable or the godmother cruel, enabled him to bring unexpected variety into his story and to challenge traditional values about the deceptive appearance of good and evil. Dickens's stories often used traditional elements, which is one of the reasons why he was and is a popular writer, but the way in which he developed and transformed them helps to explain why he is a great writer.

Dickens's early novels, however, were often criticised for being undisciplined, for having too many interesting but irrelevant episodes and too many fascinating but unnecessary characters; in short, the structure of the novels was often criticised for lacking coherence. This was a problem Dickens gradually solved with increasing success from *Dombey and Son* (1848) onwards, and when he came to write *Great Expectations* (1860-1) he constructed a plot which displays an impressive mastery of form.

The story of Pip falls naturally into three parts, which display a kind of progression from the first stages of a child's self-awareness to his mature acceptance of the human condition as a result of the experience described in the novel. Dickens clearly makes these three parts by telling us at the end of Chapter 19 that 'This is the end of the First Stage of Pip's expectations', and by telling us at the end of Chapter 39 that 'This is the end of the Second Stage of Pip's expectations'; and the book ends with Chapter 59. The story thus falls into three sections of approximately equal length – Stage 1 consisting of nineteen chapters, Stage 2 of twenty chapters, and Stage 3 of twenty chapters. In the First Stage of Pip's career, furthermore, the emphasis is upon Pip's boyhood in the countryside of the marshes; in the Second Stage we see Pip enjoying his youth in the city of London and gradually losing his moral values; and in the Third Stage Pip returns to his birthplace, abandons his false expectations, and finally becomes a mature human being.

In addition to this broad division of the novel into three stages, however, Dickens used such literary devices as parallelisms, repetitions of scene and character, and thematic variations, with such an amazing skill that, while the structure of the novel is basically simple, with fewer subplots and minor characters than in earlier works, the variations Dickens introduces keep the structure of this novel both tight and yet constantly stimulating. One illustration of the way Dickens repeats formal elements of the plot can be seen in the parallels and contrasts between the first six chapters of the novel, the beginning of the First Stage, and chapters 40-46, the first six chapters of the Third Stage. The common factor in each of these sections is Pip's encounter with Magwitch, first when he is a terrified small boy on the marshes, and then when he becomes a prosperous young man living in London. What is interesting about these two episodes, which

have such a common focus, is the difference between them, particularly
the differences in Pip's situation and in his attitude towards the ex-convict
when he meets him for the second time.

In a brilliant article in *English Literary History* (volumes 21, 1954)
J. H. Hagan has suggested that in Stage Three of *Great Expectations*
Dickens deliberately rounds off the novel, not only by resolving the
problems with which it began, but by arranging his resolutions in the very
same order as that in which the problems were presented in the First Stage
of the novel.

Thus in Chapters 1-6 Dickens deals with Pip's first meeting with
Magwitch in the churchyard; in Chapters 7-11 he introduces Pip to Miss
Havisham and Estella at Satis House but keeps the nature of Estella's
relationship to her a secret; in Chapters 12-17 Dickens deals with the
formation of Pip's ambition; and finally in Chapters 18-19 Dickens shows
Pip leaving Joe and the forge for London. As a result of these experiences
Pip's personality begins to develop in particular ways; he forms the passion-
ate desire to become a gentleman and to marry Estella.

In the Third Stage of the novel, however, Dickens, having shown us
how Pip's hopes were built up, now shows the reader how they are broken
down in a series of episodes which repeat the sequence of those in the
First Stage but with many differences of content. Thus in Chapters 40-46
Dickens deals with Pip's reunion with Magwitch, but now reveals that
Magwitch is Pip's real benefactor, not Miss Havisham as he had previously
thought. In Chapters 47-51 Pip revisits Miss Havisham, but now discovers
Estella's real identity as the daughter of Magwitch and Molly; and in
Chapters 52-56 Pip reverses the moral decline shown in Chapters 12-17,
by trying to help Herbert Pocket and by showing a marvellous concern
for Magwitch; and in Chapters 57-59 Pip leaves London and returns to
his old home on the marshes, a chastened but wiser person.

This use of repetition of episodes, particularly in the first and third
parts of the novel, is supported by the parallels between different characters
in the story. Thus, though the novel focuses upon Pip's great expectations,
he is not the only person to have ambition, and other characters who are
ambitious are compared with Pip and shown to be affected in different
ways. Pip's great expectations make him arrogant and ungrateful at times;
Pumblechook's hopes for a share of Pip's fortune make him excessive in
his congratulations; Wopsle hopes to revive the Drama and makes a fool
of himself; Sarah Pocket and Camilla expect to be named in Miss Havisham's
will, and are torn by jealousy; and Mrs Pocket's hopes for aristocratic
defence lead her to ignore domestic reality. Indeed one might say that
few in the novel other than Joe escape being affected by ambition in some
way or other, for even apparently disillusioned people such as Magwitch

and Miss Havisham hope for something as they seek to manipulate Pip and Estella.

On a smaller scale, questions about the nature of a true gentleman are also raised by a number of characters who aspire to that condition in the novel, and in their different ways Pip and Joe, Bentley Drummle and Startop, Compeyson and Mr Pocket all tell us something about the virtues of being a gentleman.

The use of repetition and contrast goes beyond the symmetrical episodes of Stages 1 and 3 or the cross-groupings of parallel characters, for the novel abounds in scenes and episodes which repeat and echo earlier ones. In Chapter 10, for example, Pip sees the secret-looking stranger stirring his drink with a file at *The Three Jolly Bargemen* public house, and discovers that he is acting on behalf of Magwitch. In Chapter 18 a scene very similar to that of Chapter 10 is described, with the same public house and a stranger talking to Joe and to Wopsle, but this time the stranger is Mr Jaggers bringing news that Pip has great expectations, and we discover that he is another agent acting on behalf of Magwitch, though Pip does not know this yet. What the scene does, of course, as well as carrying the story forward, is to point to the contrast between Pip, the boy of Chapter 10, and Pip the discontented apprentice of Chapter 18.

Other repeated incidents or scenes in the novel include the interview between Pip and Biddy in Chapter 17 and after Mrs Joe's funeral in Chapter 35, Pip's visits to Wemmick's Castle in Chapters 25 and 37 and to Jaggers's house in Soho in Chapters 26 and 48. Pip's journeys from London to Miss Havisham in Chapters 29 and 49 illustrate the changes that are taking place in Miss Havisham as well as in Pip, of course, while the two meetings between Pip and Joe in London emphasise changes in Pip's character more, the difference between Pip's irritation with Joe at the first encounter and his grateful affection at the second being especially striking.

One of the most amusing ways Dickens uses the device of repetition lies in his treatment of Mr Wopsle, the parish clerk who has theatrical ambitions, and, like Pip, goes up to London to fulfil them. When Herbert and Pip go to the theatre to see Wopsle in what turns out to be a disastrous production of *Hamlet* in Chapter 31 Pip's own hopes are still high, but when he sees Wopsle act again in Chapter 47 not only is Wopsle's dramatic career in decline, but with the return of Magwitch Pip's own hopes have been dashed, too, and we see the failure of his expectations.

The most moving use of repetition in the novel comes at the end when Pip discovers the widowed Estella in the garden of Miss Havisham's ruined house. The power and the pathos of this episode derive not merely from the situation itself but from the fact that it reminds the reader of many earlier incidents of similar but slightly different character. We remember the young Pip first meeting the beautiful young girl Estella, so proud and haughty, in Chapter 8. We remember Pip's first innocent kiss of Estella after he fought Herbert in the garden in Chapter 11. We remember their walk in the garden again in Chapter 29 when Pip was a young gentleman of great expectations, and Estella, a beautiful young woman, looked back on their pasts. Now, in Chapter 59, they have both been hurt and disappointed, and their great expectations and their youth have slipped away like the mists in the garden where they walk. We cannot help remembering their pasts as we think about their future.

The revised ending of *Great Expectations* has not received universal praise, however, and controversy about its suitability has continued from its very first appearance to the present day. The original ending of the novel came in Chapter 58 where, after the paragraph praising Herbert's industry, the matter of Chapter 59 continued with Pip's talking to Biddy. When she asked him, 'You are sure you don't fret for her?' Pip replied, 'I am sure and certain Biddy'. In a final paragraph Pip then told the reader how two years later he saw Estella again. (He had heard in the meanwhile that she had left her first husband, Bentley Drummle, who had mistreated her, and after his death, married again.) In London one day a servant brings a message saying that a lady in a nearby carriage wished to speak to him, and he and Estella greeted each other sadly. They shake hands and talk briefly before parting, though Pip felt Estella's suffering had made her more understanding than she used to be.

After the book was finished but not yet published, Dickens was persuaded by his friend Bulwer Lytton to change the ending to the one we have now. Pip leaves Biddy for a walk in the garden of Satis House, where he meets Estella; there is a reconciliation, and they leave the garden holding hands.

Dickens's great friend Forster preferred the original ending of the novel as more appropriate for Pip's sad story, and Bernard Shaw, the dramatist and one of Dickens's greatest admirers, also argued that since the book is too serious to be 'a trivially happy one', 'the conventional happy ending is an outrage on it'.

Great Expectations is essentially a developmental novel, however, in which Pip behaves badly but learns from his mistakes and his sufferings and comes to a maturity and self-knowledge. (The same is true of Estella to a lesser degree.) In a richly symbolic and schematic novel such as *Great Expectations* it can be argued that the reunion of Pip and Estella is a fitting and a powerful way of symbolising their arrival at maturity. The end of the novel does not actually describe their marriage, and there is even a hint of ambiguity about the book's last phrase, 'I saw no shadow of another parting from her', as if Pip and Estella, though coming together as friends, did not actually achieve a permanent relationship. The reader is invited to draw his or her own conclusions about their future.

Apart from the controversy about the revised ending, the other question raised about Dickens's plotting of *Great Expectations* concerns his use of coincidence, such as the way Pip, who has helped Magwitch early in the novel, should later meet and love Estella, only to discover that she is the daughter of Magwitch! Dickens himself defended this kind of unusual occurrence on the grounds that life itself is full of coincidences, and a real-life novel would therefore not be true to life unless it contained them. (When the Russian novelist Dostoevsky was writing *Crime and Punishment* a murder was committed in Russia just like the one described in his book!) Another way of dealing with the use of coincidences, and they are common in much Victorian fiction, is to ask what kind of story the writer is telling and what effect the coincidence has in the story. Dickens's novels, as we have seen, often have a fairy-tale structure, and this is particularly obvious in *Great Expectations* with its use of such *motifs* as the honest apprentice, the ugly monster, the beautiful princess and the fairy godmother. In this kind of story unexpected happenings such as coincidences seem a much more acceptable part of the fabulous atmosphere than in, for example, the more meticulously realistic novels of Jane Austen where such coincidences would make a more grating impression on the reader. The fact that Pip meets and falls in love with Estella, not knowing that she is the daughter of the convict he helped years earlier, also helps Dickens to make a point about how human lives and relationships are inextricably connected. Dickens wants the reader to feel that Pip can never entirely escape from the consequences of his past actions, and by showing us how Pip's encounter with Magwitch has repercussions on so many people in the novel, including his love-affair with Estella, he makes this view quite clear.

4.2 NARRATIVE TECHNIQUE

In writing *Great Expectations* Dickens deliberately uses the technique of a first-person narrator, that is to say, the story is ostensibly told by the hero of the novel as a kind of autobiography rather than by Dickens himself. This gives the writer certain advantages, as the reader is more likely to become directly involved in the events of a story told in this way than if the author intervenes between the reader and the events described. The reader is also able to consider the events told him by the narrator and make up his own mind about how to interpret them without necessarily agreeing with the narrator's interpretation. Even on a first reading of *Great Expectations*, for example, the reader is able to see some of the mistakes Pip is making in his growing snobbery much earlier than does Pip himself.

Dickens is, in fact extraordinarily skilful in his use of the first-person technique in the novel. The style of language the narrator uses is far more restrained than in many of Dickens's other novels. Though there are occasionally unusual images such as the description of Joe's holding his hat carefully 'like a bird's-nest with eggs in it', the language is usually lucid and direct without unnecessary elaboration, as is appropriate for the kind of person the narrator is.

The narrator is, of course, neither the boy Pip nor the youthful Mr Pip, but Mr. Pirrip, a moderately successful middle-aged businessman. Now home from overseas, he is retelling some of the crucial events of his life many years after they happened. Unlike the boy Pip, he is mature and sober, though he has a keen sense of the comic and the dramatic. In some ways he cannot now understand the kind of person the boy Pip was, and can only describe some events from memory without explaining them. Thus the diction he uses and the insights he reveals are not those of a seven-year-old boy nor of a blacksmith's apprentice but those of an intelligent and educated middle-aged man. There is generally a use of the past tense to describe events in the past, and of the present or future tenses when Mr Pirrip is talking about himself now. Almost any chapter combines the present and the past, as Mr Pirrip in the present sets the scene and then plunges the reader into it. The description of the Christmas meal in Chapter 4, for example, opens with a paragraph from the adult point-of-view, which is followed by three paragraphs in which the boy Pip is dramatically re-created in the kitchen, being harrassed by Mrs Joe. There is thus nearly always distance in the novel between Mr Pirrip, the narrator, and Pip or Mr Pip, the subject of the narration. This often enables Mr Pirrip to present episodes amusingly which were actually very painful to Pip at the time, such as when he is being bullied by Mrs Joe or Uncle Pumblechook. Generally, Dickens handles the point of view of the first-person narration with extraordinary skill in *Great Expectations*.

Though the story is ostensibly told by Mr Pirrip, however, and he is presented as a modest and mature narrator without any great extravagances of style or language, the real author of *Great Expectations* was, of course, Charles Dickens, and though he modified his language to make it as far as possible the kind of language Mr Pirrip would use, there are numerous elements in the story – symbolism, comedy, the grotesque, and many literary patterns, that are characteristic of novels written by the novelist Dickens and not simply by the fictitious character Mr Pirrip.

The story is dramatically very exciting, of course, from the opening scene in the churchyard to the final reunion with Estella, taking in, along the way, such incidents as the unexpected legacy, the return of Magwitch, the fire at Miss Havisham's, the attack on Pip by Orlick, and the desperate attempt to save Magwitch's life by rowing him down river.

Different from the purely exciting, however, is the way Dickens was able to describe certain incidents, places and people so as to arouse a mixture of feelings of fear, fascination and even some humour. The grotesque description of Miss Havisham and her house is an extremely powerful one, with the decay, the spiders and the darkness all creating feelings of fear, while at the same time the reader, like the boy Pip, is held fascinated by the extraordinary absurdity of Miss Havisham's behaviour. Magwitch, too, at least until the final stages of the novel, is a Dickensian grotesque, certainly a frightening and terrifying figure when he first leaps out at Pip, but also capable of arousing the reader's sympathy at his plight and amusement at his threats of his dreadful young man.

While not one of his most humorous works, *Great Expectations* also contains some characteristic examples of Dickens's comic genius, though all or almost all of them are fully related to the serious concerns of the novel. Wemmick, for example, with his cottage elaborately designed to look like a gothic castle, is often taken to be no more than a typically Dickensian eccentric, but the comedy of his home and his behaviour at home reveal a good deal about the way he tries to keep his private life separate from his life at the office. The account of Uncle Pumblechook is a good example of Dickens's ability to say a lot about personality without going into lengthy descriptions, and Pumblechook's calculating and pompous character is brilliantly revealed by the comic scenes in which he escorts Pip on his first visit to Satis House, teaching him mental arithmetic all the way, and by his insistence on shaking Pip's hand so frequently in order to congratulate him on his great expectations later. Trabb's boy only appears very briefly in the novel but adds to its comic effects by the way he treats Pip in Chapters 19 and 30, and yet by his impertinence the shop-keeper's assistant beautifully asserts a sense of his own equality with the newly-rich blacksmith's apprentice. The accounts of Wopsle's disastrous acting career also provide light relief in the novel, but these clearly operate as a kind of parallel to the rise and fall of Pip's own ambitions.

The ironical turns of the plot of *Great Expectations* perhaps owe something to Dickens's own familiarity with and love of the theatre. A gifted amateur actor, he also wrote plays and musical works for the stage, and although these were not particularly successful, his novels owe something to the theatre, not only in the way he handled dramatic crises, but in the remarkable way he handled dialogue. Pip's discussion with Magwitch in Chapter 3, with its flow of questions and answers is one example, while the most striking in the whole novel is probably the great quarrel between Miss Havisham and Estella in Chapter 38. This whole scene, with its careful description of the room and the protagonists' physical gestures, and the formal, rather rhetorical language –' "So proud, so proud!" moaned Miss Havisham' – shows Dickens using the conventions of the stage-play to give intensity to the episode.

Elsewhere he shows mastery of an amazing range of conversational styles from the legalistic manner of Mr Jaggers to the simple vernacular of Joe. What is particularly interesting and often moving is the way Dickens describes people with only limited powers trying to communicate. There is, for example, Joe's extraordinary conversation with Pip when he is directly addressed by Miss Havisham about Pip's apprenticeship; there is Mrs Joe's moving attempt to communicate with her family after she has been assaulted; and there is Wemmick's comic head-nodding to his deaf Aged Parent.

The names Dickens gives characters and places are often unusual, and therefore perhaps easier to remember than more commonplace names which might be forgotten between reading one instalment of the novel and the next. Some of the names, however, were clearly chosen because they suggests an additional meaning to the reader. Dickens makes this quite clear when Pip visits Miss Havisham for the first time and Estella tells him that the house is known as Satis House, which means 'enough', meaning, she said, 'that whoever had this house, could want nothing else' (Chapter 8). Though Miss Havisham has the house and money, she clearly lacks a loving husband, so we see that the name is meant ironically, as Miss Havisham's own name – 'having is a sham' – seems to be. Other names in the novel also seem to carry symbolic associations, Magwitch suggesting an evil witch, and Estella someone beautiful but remote like a star. Orlick's name seems to be an echo of the name Old Nick (or the Devil), and some readers suggest that Pip's visit to the marshes in Chapter 53 and his life-and-death struggle there with Orlick is like a journey to hell and a struggle with Satan, an encounter from which Pip emerges, as if reborn, now able to love Magwitch and to beg Joe's forgiveness. Without pressing symbolic interpretations of the novel further than the evidence will justify, the reader cannot help being aware of the ways characters and episodes in the novel contribute to the story by various means, adding to the narrative, helping to illustrate one or more of the themes, and yet providing excitement or entertainment at the same time.

Dickens often uses the repetition of references to commonplace incidents or objects as a way of adding depth to his stories, so that the contrasts between the different accounts of similar experiences enrich the reader's interpretation and enjoyment of the novel. Dickens was famous for his descriptions of food and meals, for example, and though his accounts of eating and drinking cannot be said to be symbolic in *Great Expectations* their very frequency in the novel helps the reader to define characters and their personalities. Thus Magwitch's ravenous devouring of Pip's piece of bread in the opening chapter tells us something of his desperate need, while the ruined Christmas meal in Chapter 4 tells us about Pip's relations and the values they believe in. The tragedy of Miss Havisham's ruined hopes is brilliantly brought home by the decay of her wedding-meal, and Herbert's delicacy and good manners are suggested by his gentle advice to Pip about the use of knife and spoon in Chapter 22.

Descriptions of new clothes are also used by Dickens as a suggestive way of commenting upon character. When Pip comes into his fortune and orders a new suit from Trabb, for example, this is clearly part of the larger transformation into a gentleman Pip wishes to achieve, and it is significant that Trabb's boy nearly knocks him over with his sweeping, as if to express his equality with Pip. Magwitch's attempt to disguise himself by a change of clothes is unsuccessful, we notice, and Joe, too, is extremely uncomfortable when he visits Pip in London wearing his 'holiday clothes'.

The most striking use of recurring references in the novel, however, is to be found in the numerous mention of hands, from the haunting description of 'the hands of dead people' who seem to clutch at Magwitch in the churchyard in the very first chapter. Mrs Joe is a bullying tyrant who brings Pip up 'by hand', and we are not surprised to find her described as 'having a heavy hand' in Chapter 2. Pip is criticised by Estella for his own 'coarse hands' in Chapter 8, and he worries about her seeing him working at the forge with black hands a little later. Estella's mother, the alleged murderess who works for Jaggers, has an immense grip in her hands, we learn, and Jaggers, of course, is always washing his hands. When Joe visits Pip in London in Chapter 27, he characteristically shakes hands with Pip as if he had been a pump. When Magwitch reappears, Pip cannot bear to touch him at first, but Magwitch dies holding Pip's hands, the hands which had been so badly burned in the fire at Satis House. This kind of systematic use is not accidental, and references to hands clearly invite associations with ideas of friendship, of honest labour, of innocence and guilt. This is not to say that Dickens used these hand-references with a consistent symbolic meaning, but that so many references help to give a unity to the novel and also acquire a weight and added meaning from the variety of their contexts and associations there. Thus Herbert Pocket's wish to re-name Pip as Handel, when he first comes to London has many resonances. The suggestion of a new name fits in with Pip's ambition to forget the past and acquire a new identity as a gentleman, but *that* name, with its punning reference to 'hand' and its association with the music of 'The Harmonious Blacksmith', links Pip firmly with his humble origins.

4.3 CHARACTERISATION

Dickens sets his characters before his readers clearly and directly, paying particular attention to the external details of a character's appearance, especially the face, the clothes and physical mannerisms. Though in some of his novels he also attempts internal analysis of a person's thoughts, feelings and motivation, generally Dickens prefers to reveal a character through the way he looks, behaves, and particularly the way he speaks. He is marvellously alert to little physical mannerisms and ways of speaking, and we get to know Dickens's characters from their behaviour over a long period of time rather than by the author's telling us all about them on their first appearance. When we first meet Magwitch in Chapter 1, for example, Dickens particularly emphasises the violence of his manner and language, but also draws our attention to the misery of his condition, lame and smothered in mud. Later events help us to reach a fuller understanding of his complicated personality and the reason for it.

Dickens presents his characters with varying degrees of complexity – they are not given equal treatment of space – and in a famous formulation E. M. Forster in *Aspects of the Novel* tried to distinguish between those characters presented with some degree of complexity which he called 'round', and those presented as 'flat' characters, which are constructed round a single idea of quality. In *Great Expectations*, for example, we might say that Pip is a complicated or 'round' character because he is a mixture of good and bad qualities, while Mrs Pocket is a 'flat' character, whose single characteristic is a kind of snobbish incompetence. Forster's suggestion has often led to misunderstandings, however. Nearly all literature presents characters who are developed in very varying degrees; even in Shakespeare's greatest plays minor characters such as Pistol and Bardolph lack the richness of Falstaff. But even minor, apparently 'flat' characters may have an important functional role in the novel, as Mrs Pocket helps to illustrate one of Dickens's major themes, that of false gentility, and 'flat' characters may also be rather more complicated than a simple stereotyping formula might suggest. How much of Mrs Pocket's character is the result of the way her father brought her up, for instance?

One of the most important aspects of Dickens's characterisation is the way he shows characters developing as the story proceeds. He takes a dynamic view of human personality, in other words, and though some characters such as Joe, Drummle and Compeyson may not change very much, others do remarkably. The novel concentrates particularly on Pip's moral development, of course, but Magwitch and Estella both soften in their feelings before the novel ends, Miss Havisham repents of the wrongs she has done, and even Mrs Joe shows signs of reformation.

Pip

Since the story of Pip's developing character is the main way by which Dickens articulates the central theme of *Great Expectations*, the reader should read this section in conjunction with the more detailed study of Pip's development in the section 'Themes and Issues'.

From notes Dickens left with the manuscript of the novel, we know that Pip is 'about 7 at the opening of the story'. He is brought up by his older sister as his parents and other relations are all dead. A bright and lively child, as we can see from the way he learns to read and write with such poor teaching, Pip is also very sensitive and imaginative, able to fancy what his dead brothers were like from the shape of their gravestones, capable of making up extraordinary stories about Miss Havisham later, and fond of the theatre when he grows up.

All through his life, furthermore, Pip loves deeply and attracts great love. Despite various fluctuations in his feelings, he is deeply fond of Joe and Biddy, Herbert and Wemmick, passionately in love with Estella, and most movingly grows to love Magwitch. This love is nearly always returned, consistently by Joe and Biddy, more gradually by Herbert and Wemmick, perhaps. Magwitch grows into a fatherly love of Pip, and Estella is able to love him too by the end of the story.

Pip's sensitive and loving nature is deeply affected by the harsh circumstances of his early environment, however. The death of his parent, the frequent bullying by his sister Mrs Joe and by Uncle Pumblechook and the cruel attitude of the young Estella all help to give him feelings of guilt and insecurity, feelings exaggerated by his anxiety about stealing food for the escaped convict, by telling lies about Miss Havisham and for fighting Herbert, as well as having some responsibility for the attack on Mrs Joe.

In these circumstances Pip begins to long to escape from his bleak life on the marshes and become a gentleman. When the financial help of Magwitch makes this possible and Pip goes to London at the age of 18, his ambitions lead him to behave foolishly and snobbishly for a time. He shows ingratitude to Joe, and prefers the praise of Uncle Pumblechook and Trabb. In London he spends his time in idleness and dissipation, and is so extravagant that he frequently gets into debt. When Magwitch reappears, Mr Pip, now a gentleman of twenty-three, tries to rebuff him.

But Pip's good qualities have never completely disappeared. The fact that he felt guilty about his neglect of Joe shows that he did continue to love him, and he also tried to use some of his money to help his friend Herbert. His feelings of repugnance for Magwitch soon turn to feelings of love and loyalty.

Despite an apparent timidity of character, furthermore, Pip shows a good deal of practical courage. He does help Magwitch at the beginning of the novel, partly out of fear, it is true, but he shows a great deal of resourcefulness in the plan to help Magwitch escape down river at the end. In the fight with Herbert when a boy, in rescuing Miss Havisham from the fire, and in the encounter with Orlick later, Pip also shows unexpected physical courage for someone normally very diffident and unsure of himself.

Perhaps the bravest thing Pip does in the novel, however, is to return to the marshes at the end to beg Joe's forgiveness.

Magwitch

On his first appearance, starting up from among the graves of the local churchyard, Magwitch terrifies Pip. The escaped convict has a striking presence, giving an impression of both strength and wildness, and he uses violent language too. He has 'large brown veinous hands' (Chapter 39) and usually devours his food ravenously like an animal. The name Magwitch itself, suggesting associations with black magic, adds to this impression, and in Chapter 40 Pip even compares Magwitch to the monster in Mary Shelley's novel *Frankenstein*.

Dickens makes his readers modify this hostile view of Magwitch, however, first of all by drawing attention to his pitiable condition and then by showing his gratitude to Pip for the way he helps him, and by trying to absolve him of any blame for the theft of the food in Chapter 5. He later shows more gratitude by sending Pip two pound notes, and ultimately by providing Pip with enough money to make him a gentleman.

The most powerful way by which Dickens affects the reader's attitude towards Magwitch, however, is by the gradual revelation of the harsh circumstances of Magwitch's life, deserted by his parents when very young and forced to steal turnips to keep alive. The story of his life with Estella's mother and of the way he was tricked by Compeyson also makes us more sympathetic towards him. His Christian name of Abel reminds us of the innocent man murdered by his brother Cain in the Bible, and this, too, helps to transform the reader's perception of Magwitch from that of a villain-monster to a kind-hearted man who has been ill used.

Magwitch's behaviour also softens in the later stages of the story, as Herbert and Pip both notice. He begins to love Pip for what Pip feels and does for him rather than because he has made Pip into a gentleman. It is impossible for the reader not to feel love and pity for Magwitch in Chapters 54, 55 and 56.

The reader is still forced to ask questions about Magwitch's behaviour, about his thieving, forgery and violence, and about his motives in using his money to make Pip a gentleman, but most readers will feel Magwitch in the end was more sinned against than sinning.

Joe Gargery

Joe Gargery is Pip's brother-in-law and the village blacksmith. He has fair hair and blue eyes, and is very strong as befits his occupation, able to stand up to everyone in the village and even give Orlick a beating.

Despite his strength, however, Joe is normally kind and gentle, 'a mild, good-natured, sweet-tempered, easy-going, foolish, dear fellow', as Pip describes him in Chapter 2, 'a sort of Hercules in strength and also in weakness'.

Partly because of his upbringing and lack of education, Joe lacks sophistication and social ease. He is virtually illiterate at the beginning of the novel, finds it difficult to talk to Miss Havisham in Chapter 13, and is very uncomfortable when he makes his first visit to Pip in London. He nearly always behaves awkwardly when away from the forge or in his holiday clothes, looking 'more like a scarecrow in good circumstances, than anything else', when dressed for the Christmas meal in Chapter 4.

Joe's lack of social skills is more than compensated for by his moral qualities, however, which are so attractive that many readers feel he is virtually the moral touchstone in the novel, against whom all the other characters have to be measured. He is generous and loving, especially towards Pip, shows pity to Magwitch, fairness to Orlick, and toleration of his wife's nagging. He has a strong sense of the virtue of industry and possesses a simple dignity in a world which abounds in snobbery and wordly ambition.

His toleration of his wife's bullying of Pip does raise questions, however. In Chapter 7 Joe explains that he would rather suffer Mrs Joe's behaviour than crush her, as his father did his mother, and in Chapter 57 he regrets that he was not able to give Pip more protection from Mrs Joe, but says his interventions only made matters worse. But Joe was able to deal with his wife on occasions, over the quarrel with Orlick and in reporting Miss Havisham's gift, where he displays both firmness and sensitivity. It is for the reader to decide how serious this weakness to protect Pip is in Joe's essentially lovable character.

Mrs Joe Gargery

Mrs Joe is aged about thirty when the novel begins because we know that she is more than twenty years older than Pip and he is about seven. In appearance she is tall and bony, with black hair and eyes, and a skin so red that Pip sometimes wonders whether she washed with a nutmeg-grater instead of soap! She almost always wears a coarse apron with a square bib in front so full of pins and needles that they sometimes get into the bread she is cutting!

The apron, in fact, is almost a clue to Mrs Joe's personality, which is dominated by a spiky passion for cleanliness and respectability. She is always cleaning the house, and trying to do her best for Pip and her husband by such activities as preaching good behaviour, dosing them with medicine, and vigorously pursuing their interests. The trouble is that she is so narrow-minded in her interpretation of those interests and so physically unpleasant in her manners towards Pip and Joe that her cleanliness and morality are harsh and tyrannical. She is often on the rampage with her wax-ended tickler and she rarely stops nagging. The meals in her house are ordeals rather than occasions for family happiness.

Because of her strong and dominant personality she probably has the crucial influence on Pip's boyhood, creating his early feelings of guilt and inadequacy. It is she, too, who encourages Pip to have great expectations of Miss Havisham, and is thus responsible for much of Pip's unhappy later development.

Her hard and unfeeling treatment of Orlick produces unexpected results, however, for he resents her behaviour and assaults her brutally, causing her to lose her power of speech. Though she never completely recovers her health, there are signs at the end of Chapter 16 that she recognises the wrong she did Orlick and wants a reconciliation. When Biddy describes Mrs Joe's death in Chapter 35, furthermore, it is clear that Mrs Joe recognised the wrongs she did Pip and her husband, and she asked to be forgiven. Pip is not the only character in the novel who has grown in moral understanding by the end of the story.

Miss Havisham

Though the idea for the character of Miss Havisham may have been suggested to Dickens by stories of real people, his presentation of her in the novel is less rounded, less realistic, than that of other characters, such as Pip. Her role in the novel seems to be more functional and symbolic, suggesting a certain kind of response to unhappiness. Thus both her own name and that of her house punningly draw attention to the fact that having great wealth may not be enough to guarantee happiness. Miss Havisham's decision to keep all her clocks permanently stopped at twenty minutes to nine, and to continue to wear her wedding-dress are Dickens's very effective way of showing the reader how Miss Havisham attempts to reject the real world and to stop time.

Dickens is, however, telling a story which is broadly realistic, so he does present Miss Havisham with many recognisably human features. Her appearance in white satin, lace and silk is elaborately described in Chapter 8, as the young Pip notices how faded and yellow the wedding attire has become. Though she is not so very old, fifty-six in the third part of the novel, she seems more elderly than she is, and uses a crutch to walk with.

The reason for Miss Havisham's extraordinary way of life is gradually revealed, first by Herbert's revelation of the way she was jilted on her wedding-day in Chapter 22, and then by Magwitch's account of Compeyson's deliberate swindling of her in Chapter 42. These two retrospective explanations help to make Miss Havisham' behaviour more realistic and pitiable, of course.

She is nevertheless for Pip virtually his 'fairy godmother', and so he thinks of her in Chapter 19, when he believes she is the rich person whose wealth is to help him become a gentleman. She had, after all, introduced him to Estella and paid Joe £25 for his apprenticeship. Pip had also met the lawyer, Mr Jaggers, at her house, so his error is not too difficult to understand.

Miss Havisham is not Pip's fairy godmother, however. Hurt by Compeyson's cruel treatment of her, she deliberately adopted the very young Estella and brought her up to win the love of men whom she could then humiliate as revenge for the pain Miss Havisham suffered. She wished to use Estella and other people as she herself was used, and, far from being a fairy godmother, proves to be more like a wicked witch.

Miss Havisham's plans do not work out. By Chapter 38 she realises that in bringing up Estella to love no one, she has also lost Estella's love for her. Realising the harm she has done, she shows signs of regret and helps Pip in his plan to assist Herbert's business career. Lonely and almost broken by remorse, she begs Pip's forgiveness in Chapter 49 and her death by fire symbolises the death of her old revengeful character. Later we learn that she also followed Pip's advice and left Matthew Pocket a substantial fortune in her will.

Estella

Estella's name derives from the Latin word for a star, and her appearance has something of a star's beauty as her character has something of its remoteness.

When Pip first meets her he immediately notices her pretty brown hair and her assured manner, though she is in fact about the same age he is. She has been adopted and brought up by Miss Havisham, and despises the coarse ways of the common labouring boy Pip, but he falls in love with her.

Mr Jaggers explains Estella's early history to Pip in Chapter 51; she is the daughter of Magwitch and Molly, whom Jaggers succeeded in having acquitted from a murder charge, and he then arranged for her to be adopted by Miss Havisham.

Miss Havisham brings Estella up to become a beautiful, educated and proud young woman, so that men will fall in love with her, but she will not be able to return their love. (In this way Miss Havisham hopes to obtain revenge for the wrongs done to *her*.)

Estella is perfectly honest with Pip about this. She repeatedly warns him that she has no heart or softness. In fact, her honesty with Pip shows that he is the one person, apart from Miss Havisham, for whom she has any regard whatsoever. Despite these warnings, however Pip continues to fall more and more in love with her.

Estella's truthfulness leads her in Chapter 38 to tell Miss Havisham she cannot feel gratitude to her because that is the way Miss Havisham brought her up – and then Miss Havisham begins to realise the harm she has done. Estella continues to behave in the way she has been trained, however. She flirts with Bentley Drummle, though she knows this gives Pip pain, and eventually marries him. But the marriage proves to be a disaster. Drummle treats her with great cruelty and eventually she leaves him.

The experience of these terrible years changes Estella. Though still attractive, she loses the freshness of her beauty; her proud eyes become softer and the touch of her hand friendlier. She has learned from her sufferings, too, and has become a wiser person, better able to understand Pip. It seems as if they will be able to achieve a loving relationship at the end of the novel.

Mr Jaggers

Mr Jaggers is a burly, dark man with a large head which is bald on top. He has sharp and suspicious eyes and bushy black eyebrows, but his most striking physical features, frequently referred to are his large hands which smell of scented soap.

He is the lawyer who deals with Miss Havisham's business affairs, and Pip first meets him at Satis House. This meeting is one of the main reasons why Pip comes to believe that Miss Havisham is the source of his expectations. Only later does Pip discover that Mr Jaggers is also Magwitch's legal representative. Jaggers is evidently a very able lawyer and much in demand for his services. His skill is largely responsible for Molly's acquittal from a murder charge.

Being a lawyer has had a powerful influence on Jaggers's character, however. First of all, he is very forceful and yet precise in his speech, browbeating Mr Wosple in Chapter 18, for example. He is always anxious not to be understood to have said or implied more than he intends. Secondly, there are signs that he is not over-scrupulous in his legal practice, and he is willing to use bribed witnesses as long as he does not know the exact nature of their perjury, as we see in Chapter 20. Thirdly, he tends to enjoy the power his legal reputation has earned him, and often bullies his clients or treats them harshly. Wemmick's account of the way no one would dare steal Jaggers's gold watch is an illustration of his hold over criminals. Finally, though Jaggers seems to deal with his clients in a bluff and hearty manner, the fact that he is always washing his hands suggests that he feels tainted by his work and wants to remove traces of it in much the same way as Lady Macbeth goes on trying to wash off the evidence of Duncan's murder long after the real blood has disappeared from her hands. There is a particularly vivid account of Jaggers's handwashing after a case 'of a darker complexion than usual' at the beginning of Chapter 26.

Beneath his formidable and suspicious exterior, however, Jaggers does possess kindly feelings, as Pip discovers towards the end of the story when Jaggers reveals how he not only defended Molly but went out of his way to arrange for Molly's child to be adopted by Miss Havisham. He does his best for Magwitch, too, at the end, but generally seems ashamed to reveal any tender feelings, preferring to hide them behind a legalistic and bullying manner.

Mr Wopsle

Mr Wopsle is clerk at the village church on the marshes, the person who would help the clergyman during services by leading the congregation in the responses. A regular visitor to Pip's household, he has a Roman nose and a large, shining forehead, and is particularly proud of his deep voice which he uses to great effect in church.

He is not as hypocritical as Uncle Pumblechook, and is friendly towards Pip, but he is generally presented as a comic figure. His role in the novel is perhaps mainly functional in that he exists primarily to contribute to the plot and its thematic interests rather than to be a character in his own right.

He is ambitious and would like to have achieved success in the Church. He is extremely proud of his voice and very fond of using it to theatrical effect, quoting Shakespeare, reciting poetry, and even giving a memorable reading of a murder trial from a newspaper one evening in *The Jolly Bargemen*.

Believing that he has great expectations of reviving the Drama and of becoming a successful actor, Mr Wopsle turns professional and goes to London, where he gives a comically disastrous performance of *Hamlet*, which is described in Chapter 31; he soon descends to performing in a rather poor Christmas pantomime.

Mr Wopsle's career, in other words, repeats on a smaller scale the career of Pip. Both journey from the marshes to London; both have great hopes; and both see their expectations disappointed. It is no coincidence that Pip witnesses the decline of Wopsle's theatrical ambitions in Chapter 47 immediately after the return of Magwitch has shatted his own ambitions.

Wopsle's insistence on reading Pip the tragedy of George Barnwell in Chapter 15 is another ironical episode in their relationship. This once-famous eighteenth-century play is about an unhappy but ambitious young apprentice who murders his master, and, though Wopsle's motives for reading are partly out of personal vanity, the story of the play is another faint echo of Pip's own situation.

Uncle Pumblechook

Uncle Pumblechook is Joe Gargery's uncle, and a well-to-do corn chandler and seed merchant. A hard-breathing, middle-aged man, he has a disagreeable appearance with a fish-like mouth, dull, staring eyes, and sandy hair which stands upright on his head.

Though he likes to be thought generous, he is in fact extremely unpleasant. He bullies Pip, always urging him to be grateful for what small mercies he receives from his sister, and insisting the small boy should practise mental arithmetic all the way to Miss Havisham's. He enjoys flattery and pretends to have knowledge he does not have – when Pip first visits Miss Havisham's house, for example and again when Miss Havisham pays for Pip's apprenticeship.

Pumblechook's character is not fully drawn, however, and he can perhaps best be described by the single word 'hypocrite'. After bullying Pip in his childhood, his attitude changes to one of obsequiousness when Pip comes into money. His constant shaking of Pip's hand in Chapter 19, usually preceded by the catchphrase 'May I?' is one of the best comic episodes in the novel. His claim to have been Pip's benefactor is a recurring feature in the book's later stages, until Pip denounces him, and then he promptly accuses Pip of 'ingratitoode'. He is incorrigible, and few readers will not be amused when they learn of what Orlick did to him!

Compeyson

Pip first sees Compeyson, though he does not know him by that name at the time, when he takes food to the escaped convict in the churchyard in Chapter 3, and there startles another escaped criminal. Though Compeyson is dressed in coarse grey clothes and with a leg iron like Magwitch, Pip is able to identify him by the bruise on the left side of his face.

Gradually, from the accounts of him given by Herbert Pocket in Chapter 22 and by Magwitch in Chapter 42, the reader is able to piece together some of Compeyson's history. Educated at a public school and smooth-talking, Compeyson looks and behaves like a gentleman, but is in fact an accomplished criminal, an expert forger and swindler. Through his acquaintance with her half-brother, Arthur, Compeyson embezzled large sums of money from Miss Havisham and promised to marry her, but then jilted her on the wedding-day. Compeyson took Magwitch as his accomplice, and, though younger than Magwitch, thoroughly exploited him. When they were both arrested, Compeyson persuaded the court, however, that Magwitch was the more guilty party and so received a lighter sentence.

Compeyson knows of Magwitch's desire for revenge, and when he discovers that Magwitch has returned from Australia does what he can to have him re-arrested, though in the attempted escape down the river it is Compeyson who is drowned.

Compeyson's character is not very fully developed. His role in the novel is mainly functional and he is very important indeed for the plot. Not only does he form one of the group of gentlemen whose characters are constantly compared with those of Pip and Joe, but if he had not been involved with Miss Havisham and Magwitch before the action of the novel began, the plot would never have taken off. Dickens finds no redeeming feature in Compeyson's character as he does in those or Magwitch and Orlick, and for this reason some readers find his presentation very melodramatic. On the other hand his character may indicate that Dickens believed there were some people for whom no extenuating circumstances could be found.

Biddy

Biddy is Mr Wopsle's great-aunt's grand-daughter, and helps her grandmother run the evening school where Pip first meets her. An orphan like Pip, she is rather bedraggled in appearance in the early days, her hair always wanting brushing and her shoes mending. She has a difficult time with her pupils to begin with.

Biddy's appearance and manner improve as she grows up, however. When Mrs Joe is assaulted, Biddy moves into Joe's household as her attendant, and she soon reveals her shrewd and caring nature. In better circumstances her appearance improves too, and she becomes pleasant, wholesome and sweet-tempered, with especially pretty and thoughtful eyes. She is increasingly valued by Pip for her gentle, kind and wise personality, and he wishes he could fall in love with her rather than be in love with Estella. Pip is jealous of the attention Orlick pays her, and the fact that Biddy becomes widely appreciated is shown by the fact that she gets the place of mistress in the new village school.

Biddy's main role in the novel, however, is to help reveal Pip's growing snobbery. In Chapter 17 she warns him that his longing to become a gentleman in order to win or to spite Estella is not very sensible. In Chapter 19 she defends Joe against Pip's attacks on his manners, and in Chapter 35 she gently reproaches Pip for the way he is neglecting Joe.

With the collapse of all his hopes in London, with Magwitch dead and with Estella married, Pip resolves at the end of the novel to return to the marshes, to beg the forgiveness of Biddy and Joe, and ask Biddy to marry him. Too late he discovers that Biddy has already married Joe, by whom she later has a little boy whom she called Pip.

Herbert Pocket

Pip first meets Herbert Pocket when, visiting Satis House as a young boy, he is challenged to a fight by a completely unknown pale young gentleman – they are about the same age – with red eyelids and light hair. Though Pip wins the fight, the pale young gentleman takes his defeat in good part.

Subsequently when Pip comes into his expectations and moves to London, he discovers that the person he is to share rooms with in Bernard's Inn is the same person, and they soon become close friends. Herbert is the son of Matthew Pocket, who is to be Pip's tutor, and Mrs Pocket, a rather helpless woman with aristocratic pretensions, and they are relations of Miss Havisham, though she has disowned them.

Herbert works in a counting-house, though without pay, and has great ambitions of a successful business career if he can only obtain some capital. Pip admires the way he bears his poverty, especially since he is engaged to be married to Clara Barley.

He has a frank and open manner, and though not particularly handsome is extremely amiable and cheerful. He is totally loyal to Pip, sympathises with his unhappy love-affair with Estella, and plays a willing part in the attempt to save Magwitch.

Herbert is something of a dreamer, however. It is amusingly character-istic of him that he does not remember the outcome of his fight with Pip accurately, and, though his attempts to improve Pip's manner are gently done, his wish to rename Pip 'Handel' seems somewhat unnecessary. Pip secretly helps to further Herbert's business prospects, and eventually Herbert makes a success of the firm of Clarriker and Co., but readers may still feel that Pip's final judgement of Herbert's acumen and industry is a generous one.

Dolge Orlick

Orlick only makes a few appearances in the novel – he appears or is referred to in only six chapters, in fact – but his presence is a very powerful one. Employed to help Joe Gargery in his forge, he is a broad-shouldered man of great strength, whose swarthy appearance, slouching manner and morose temperament are very alarming to the young Pip.

There are also suggestions that Orlick is more than disagreeable, however. He is often referred to as 'Old Orlick', a phrase which sounds like the popular name for the Devil of 'Old Nick'. In Chapter 15 Pip says that Orlick claimed 'he knew the fiend very well', and the description of him at work in the forge is not unlike a description of a devil in hell.

Orlick's deeds are also very vicious. He brutally assaults Miss Joe with a treacherous blow on the back of her head, and later lures Pip down to an old sluice-house, on the marshes where he nearly kills him in another scene with diabolic overtones. He makes unwelcome advances to Biddy, and the very last time that we hear of him he is in jail for robbery.

Yet Dickens qualifies any simplistic interpretation of Orlick as Evil incarnate. It is significant that Joe Gargery, though he fights Orlick for insulting his wife, does give him a half-day holiday and share a pot of beer with him as if he is not wholly unsympathetic. Even Mrs Joe shows signs of forgiving him for his attack on her, and the account of Orlick's robbery of Uncle Pumblechook in Chapter 57 is surely comic rather than macabre.

Although Orlick is violent, the reader cannot help wondering whether Pip, who is the source of most information about Orlick, may not have some responsibility for his behaviour. There are signs that Pip is jealous of him over Biddy, and his determination to get Orlick dismissed from Miss Havisham's employment also seems rather harsh. Oddest of all is Orlick's statement in Chapter 53 that it was Pip who assaulted Mrs Joe!

Orlick is very like Pip in many ways. He lives and works with Joe and his wife; he is attracted to Biddy; he knows Miss Havisham; and he also tries to help an ex-convict. In the assault on Mrs Joe and on Uncle Pumble-chook, he can be seen to be committing deeds Pip would have like to have done but for which he lacked the courage. As a result of these near-parallels, some readers have interpreted Orlick as Pip's *alter ego*, his other self, with the unrestrained power to perform deeds which Pip's nervous nature lacks. More likely Dickens sees Orlick as a contrast to Pip. Both have been brought up in a brutal and alienating society, but though Pip is bruised and almost crushed by it he survives to become a decent human being, while Orlick becomes a figure of violence.

Mr Wemmick

Mr Wemmick works as a clerk for Mr Jaggers in his law-office in Little Britain in London. A short man, he has a square, wooden face with glittering eyes – 'small, keen, and black' – and a small slit of a mouth like a letter-box. He usually wears several rings and a brooch, and when Pip first meets him he is aged between forty and fifty.

At work in the office Wemmick is brisk and efficient, but displays a good deal of cynicism about human nature. He is genuinely surprised when, for example, Pip first offers to shake hands with him, he bullies the clients, and is not above mild bribery. 'Get hold of portable property' appears to be his philosophy and he refuses to advise Pip about ways of using his money to help Herbert.

At his home in Walworth, however, Wemmick is almost the opposite. He displays great ingenuity in the design and layout of his gothic cottage and garden, and reveals a most affectionate nature in his relationship with his dead and aged father. He gradually becomes a loyal friend of Pip's, helping him to assist Herbert's business career, and proving a trustworthy ally in the plan to rescue Magwitch.

Wemmick's attempts to separate the two areas of his life, his office and his home, and the two sides of his nature, cynicism and affection, are suggested symbolically by the way in whcih Wemmick's mouth tightens as he nears Little Britain, and by the castle-like character of his home in Walworth. His behaviour also leads to some of Dickens' best comedy in the novel, for example in his apparently accidental wedding with Miss Skiffins.

Wemmick is more than a typically Dickensian comic character, however. His dual personality, although presented affectionately, reveals the way the pressures of life threaten to distort human behaviour, making kindness and integrity difficult to preserve in the world of work. (A fuller account of Pip's visit to Wemmick's house can be found in the next section.)

Bentley Drummle

Bentley Drummle is one of Pip's fellow-students whom he meets at the house of Mr Pocket in Hammersmith. He is heavy in figure and movement, with a sluggish complexion and sulky manners. He has rich relations in Somerset and is the next heir but one to a baronetcy.

Idle, proud, niggardly, reserved and suspicious, Drummle is an unlikeable character, soon nicknamed 'the Spider' by Mr Jaggers. Boastful and arrogant, he behaves boorishly when dining at the lawyer's house, but to Pip's dismay apparently wins the sympathy of Estella, and she announces their engagement in Chapter 44.

Jaggers has the measure of Drummle, however, forecasting that his marriage to Estella will be a battle of wills, and that he may well use physical violence against his wife. The forecast comes true. After the wedding Drummle does treat Estella cruelly, and she leaves him. Two years later he dies in an accident characteristically brought about by his ill-treatment of a horse.

Though Drummle's character is only sketched in and given very little complexity, he has an important role in the novel overall, not only as the major instrument in Estella's change of personality, but also as one of the group of characters illustrating the different ways of being a gentleman.

5 SPECIMEN PASSAGE AND COMMENTARY

5.1 SPECIMEN PASSAGE

Pip is living in London, learning to lead the life of a gentleman, and in this passage from Chapter 25 he accompanies his legal acquaintance, Mr Wemmick, to his home, which is in the district of Walworth:

It appeared to be a collection of back lanes, ditches, and little gardens, and to present the aspect of a rather dull retirement. Wemmick's house was a little wooden cottage in the midst of plots of garden, and the top of it was cut out and painted like a battery mounted with guns.

'My own doing,' said Wemmick. 'Looks pretty; don't it?'

I highly commended it. I think it was the smallest house I ever saw; with the queerest gothic windows (by far the greater part of them sham), and a gothic door, almost too small to get in at.

'That's a real flagstaff, you see,' said Wemmick, 'and on Sundays I run up a real flag. Then look here. After I have crossed this bridge, I hoist it up - so - and cut off the communication.'

The bridge was a plank, and it crossed a chasm about four feet wide and two deep. But it was very pleasant to see the pride with which he hoisted it up and made it fast; smiling as he did so, with a relish and not merely mechanically.

'At nine o'clock every night, Greenwich time,' said Wemmick, 'the gun fires. There he is, you see! And when you hear him go, I think you'll say he's a Stinger.'

The piece of ordnance referred to, was mounted in a separate fortress, constructed of lattice-work. It was protected from the weather by an ingenious little tarpaulin contrivance in the nature of an umbrella.

'Then, at the back,' said Wemmick, 'out of sight, so as not to impede the idea of fortifications - for it's principle with me, if you have an idea, carry it out and keep it up - I don't know whether that's your opinion - '

I said, decidedly.

' - At the back, there's a pig, and there are fowls and rabbits; then, I knock together my own little frame, you see, and grow cucumbers; and you'll judge at supper what sort of salad I can raise. So, sir,' said Wemmick, smiling again, but seriously too, as he shook his head, 'if you can suppose the little place besieged, it would hold out a devil of a time in point of provisions.'

The, he conducted me to a bower about a dozen yards off, but which was approached by such ingenious twists of path that it took quite a long time to get at; and in this retreat our glasses were already set forth. Our punch was cooling in a ornamental lake, on whose margin the bower was raised. This piece of water (with an island in the middle which might have been the salad for supper) was of a circular form, and he had constructed a fountain in it, which, when you set a little mill going and took a cork out of a pipe, played to that powerful extent that it made the back of your hand quite wet.

'I am my own engineer, and my own carpenter, and my own plumber, and my own gardener, and my own Jack of all Trades,' said Wemmick, in acknowledging my compliments. 'Well; it's a good thing, you know. It brushes the Newgate cobwebs away, and pleases the Aged. You wouldn't mind being at once introduced to the Aged, would you? It wouldn't put you out?'

I expressed the readiness I felt, and we went into the castle. There, we found, sitting by the fire, a very old man in a flannel coat, clean, cheerful, comfortable, and well cared for, but intensely deaf.

'Well aged parent,' said Wemmick, shaking hands with him in a cordial and jocose way, 'how am you?'

'All right, John; all right!' replied the old man.

'Here's Mr Pip, aged parent, 'said Wemmick,' and I wish you could hear his name. Nod away at him, Mr Pip; that's what he likes. Nod away at him, if you please, like winking!'

'This is a fine place of my son's, sir,' cried the old man, while I nodded as hard as I possibly could. 'This is a pretty pleasure-ground, sir. This spot and these beautiful works upon it ought to be kept together by the Nation, after my son's time, for the people's enjoyment.'

'You're as proud of it as Punch; ain't you, Aged?' said Wemmick, contemplating the old man, with his hard face really softened; there's a nod for you;: giving him a tremendous one; 'there's another for you;' giving him a still more tremendous one; 'you like that, don't you? If you're not tired, Mr Pip – though I know it's tiring to strangers – will you tip him one more? You can't think how it pleases him.'

I tipped him several more, and he was in great spirits. We left him bestirring himself to feed the fowls, and we sat down to our punch in the arbour; where Wemmick told me as he smoked a pipe that it had taken him a good many years to bring the property up to its present pitch of perfection.

'Is it your own, Mr Wemmick?'

'O yes, 'said Wemmick, 'I have got hold of it, a bit at a time. It's freehold, by George!'

'Is it, indeed? I hope Mr Jaggers admires it?'

'Never seen it, 'said Wemmick. 'Never heard of it. Never seen the Aged. Never heard of him. No; the office is one thing, and private life is another. When I go into the office, I leave the Castle behind me, and when I come into the Castle, I leave the office behind me. If it's not in any way disagreeable to you, you'll oblige me by doing the same. I don't wish it professionally spoken about.'

Of course I felt my good faith involved in the observance of his request. The punch being very nice, we sat there drinking it and talking, until it was almost nine o'clock. 'Getting near gun-fire, 'said Wemmick then, as he laid down his pipe; 'it's the Aged's treat.'

Proceeding into the Castle again, we found the Aged heating the poker, with expectant eyes, as a preliminary to the performance of this great nightly ceremony. Wemmick stood with his watch in his hand, until the moment was come for him to take the red-hot poker from the Aged, and repair to the battery. He took it, and went out, and presently the Stinger went off with a Bang that shook the crazy little box of a cottage as if it must fall to pieces, and made every glass and teacup in it ring. Upon this, the Aged – who I believe would have been blown out of his arm-chair but for holding on by the elbows – cried out exultingly, 'He's fired! I heard him!' and I nodded at the old gentleman until it is no figure of speech to declare that I absolutely could not see him.

5.2 CRITICAL COMMENTARY

At the time when the novel was set, Walworth was a small village in south-east London, and Pip's first impression of the district is of a rather miscellaneous collection of 'back lanes, ditches, and little gardens', a typical suburban area of the time, in fact, with little individuality. What Pip notices about Wemmick's house, first of all, is its small size and its vulner-ability – it is 'a little wooden cottage' – but he also notices that the top of the house 'was cut out and painted like a battery with guns'. Though Wemmick lives in a small cottage in the suburbs, in other words, he tries to make it look like a fortified castle. One of the key features of this whole passage is his contrast between what the house is, and what Wemmick pretends it is.

The contrast is emphasised in the third paragraph where, we are told, Wemmick's house has 'the queerest gothic windows' and 'a gothic door'. The gothic style of architecture enjoyed a revival in the nineteenth century, and Wemmick is reflecting the fashion for that style in the design of his house. What makes his ambition so comical, however, is the disparity between his wish to make his house seem like a gothic castle and its actual size, for it is, as Pip says, 'the smallest house I ever saw' with 'a gothic door almost too small to get in at'. Some of the windows are 'sham', that is, dummy windows without glass, but the word 'sham' is often used to describe something that is other than it seems.

Wemmick's attempts to give his house the appearance of a fortification are emphasised when we read that the cottage has a flagstaff with 'a real flag', a drawbridge over a moat, and a 'piece of ordnance', that is, a mounted gun, which is fired at nine o'clock every night. Yet with almost every detail Dickens makes us smile at the modesty of Wemmick's attempts, for the drawbridge is only 'a plank', the moat is only 'four feet wide', and the size of the gun is revealed by the fact that it is small enough to be protected from the weather by a sort of umbrella!

Wemmick is not really trying to turn his modest little cottage into a genuinely fortified castle, of course. He is only indulging in a harmless hobby, and he knows it. 'My own doing,' he says proudly, 'Looks pretty; don't it?' Pip's attitude to Wemmick throughout the passage is one of amused affection, not bitter satire. Pip does not dislike him as he does Compeyson or Bentley Drummle, and Wemmick indeed becomes one of Pip's closest friends.

But Dickens was a serious writer who noticed and was disturbed by various aspects of nineteenth-century English society, and by their pro-found and devastating effects upon people's lives. He often revealed a character's personality by describing features of his outward appearance, his physical mannerisms or the kind of house he lived in, rather than by trying to describe a character's inner psychological makeup. We already know a certain amount about Wemmick by this stage of the novel. He is Jaggers' clerk and deals with the criminal underworld of London; and he often seems cynical and materialistic in his dealings with people at his business office in Little Britain. Yet when Pip accompanies him home to Walworth, Pip discovers a new side to his nature.

Further details of Wemmick's character come to light when Pip discovers that he is a keen gardener, who keeps a pig, fowls and rabbits, and has built in his garden a bower (or summerhouse), an ornamental lake, and even a small fountain. Wemmick's underlying idea of viewing his home as a fortification is continued, however, with his claim that it is almost self-sufficient in providing food, for, he says, that 'if you can suppose the little place besieged, it would hold out a devil of a time in point of provision'. Though Wemmick is smiling as he says this, it is important to note that Dickens also says he was speaking 'seriously too'. At the same time, the comic side of Wemmick's ingenuity is underlined by the fact that the path to the bower is only 'a dozen yards', despite its ingenious twists, and that the fountain is so small that it only 'made the back of your hand quite wet'.

The three dominant ideas that gradually emerge from this impressively detailed account of Wemmick's home life so far then are, first, that in designing his home and garden Wemmick displays far more ingenuity and imagination than one might expect from knowing him at his office; secondly, that much of his ingenuity is devoted to redesigning his home in the style of a castle, capable of withstanding an attack or siege; and thirdly, that the final effect is comical because of the disproportion between what is designed and its ludicrously small size.

Yet far from being the dry-as-dust lawyer's clerk we might have expected, Wemmick already seems to have justified his claim to be 'my own engineer, and my own carpenter, and my own plumber, and my own gardener, and my own Jack of all Trades'. He is indeed a throughly inventive and versatile person.

This dichotomy between Wemmick, the apparently dull clerk, and Wemmick, the creative person, is ever more marked when Pip enters Wemmick's 'castle', for there he meets a very old man, but 'clean, comfortable, and well cared for'. This is Wemmick's very deaf father, and, far from being the cold and cynical character he seems at the office, Wemmick now reveals himself as a tender and loving son. His father is so deaf that conversation with him is virtually impossible; but what is impressive and moving here is the way Wemmick not only makes his father a comfortable home, but manages to keep up a cheerful relationship with him despite his deafness. He introduces Pip to him and urges Pip to communicate with his father, not by talk, which is impossible, but by a comic body language. 'Nod away at him, Mr. Pip; that's what he likes. Nod away if you please, like winking!' Dickens brilliantly conveys Wemmick's deep affection, through this apparently absurd behaviour.

The old man is proud of his son and his house – 'it ought to be kept together by the Nation, after my son's time' he says proudly, in another unconsciously comic touch. Wemmick's face, we notice, which tightens

into a letter-box when he walks back to the office next day, 'really softened' for his father here, and again he insists on drawing Pip into the
relationship with his father. He wants his father to live as normal a life as
is compatible with his age and his infirmity.

He does not merely look after his father, but tries to involve him
actively in the household by making him feel useful, and in the next
paragraph we find Wemmick's father 'bestirring himself to feed the fowls',
as Wemmick talks to Pip about his home.

Wemmick's philosophy of life now becomes quite explicit, for when
Pip asks if Mr Jaggers admires his castle, Wemmick reveals that Jaggers
knows nothing of it nor of his father. This is quite deliberate, he goes on:
'No; the office is one thing, and private life is another. When I go into the
office, I leave the Castle behind me, and when I come into the Castle, I
leave the office behind me.'

Wemmick's castle-cottage is revealed as a place where has has tried to
create a loving and creative environment for himself and his father as a
deliberate contrast to the place where he works and earns his living, where
he deals with criminals and injustices and cruelty, and where he behaves
in a hard and cynical manner. Wemmick tries, in other words, to effect a
complete separation between his business and his private life. His castle-
cottage, self-sufficient enough to be able to withstand a siege, and with
a drawbridge which can 'cut off the communication' from the outside
world, is a vivid and entertaining symbol of the way he has tried to defend
his private life.

By various deft touches, such as the references to the smallness of the
cottage, the absurdity of the moat, and the fact revealed later that the
cottage is 'subject to dry-rot', Dickens reveals, however, that Wemmick's
attempt to keep the two parts of his life separate by living in a fortified
cottage may not be completely satisfactory.

The precariousness of Wemmick's castle becomes clearer in the description of the gun-firing ceremony. It is characteristic of Wemmick's kindness
again that he involves his father in the ceremony by letting him heat the
iron poker which ignites the gunpowder. But though the small gun only
goes off with a bang, and does not discharge a cannon-ball, it is significant
(and also amusing) that its explosion 'shook the crazy little box of a
cottage as if it must fall to pieces'. Despite all Wemmick's attempts to give
his home the appearance of a fortified castle, in other words, it remains,
in a wonderfully telling phrase, 'a crazy little box of a cottage'. In the
same paragraph, Dickens also uses the word 'battery' to describe the place-
ment for the gun. It is a word we first met in the opening chapter in the
churchyard when Magwitch arranged to meet Pip at the Old Battery. One
cannot help thinking that the word is used quite deliberately again here to

remind us of the world of crime and violence against which Wemmick's home is a symbolical defence.

Wemmick is almost like a comic Jekyll and Hyde figure, with two very different sides to his character, depending on whether he is at home or in the office. Dickens brilliantly uses this minor and eccentric character not merely to enrich his story with comedy, but to suggest how some people try to cope with unpleasant aspects of life by making a separation between their public and their private lives. But in depicting the small size and the fragility of the castle, Dickens emphasises the fact that Wemmick's kind of separation is not likely to be completely satisfactory. It is no coincidence that the last time we hear the word 'castle' used in the novel is when the Joe Gargery repeats the saying that 'an Englishman's ouse is his Castle' (Chapter 57), but also reveals that Orlick has busted into and robbed Uncle Pumblechook's! Dickens's portrait of Wemmick and his home is an amusing and affectionate one, but it does question the ultimate validity of Wemmick's philosophy, though in the gentlest possible way. This is comic writing of the very highest order.

6 CRITICAL RECEPTION

Great Expectations was a great popular success with the reading public from its very first appearance on 1 December 1860, as the main serial story in Dickens's own weekly journal *All The Year Round*. The circulation of the periodical had been falling during the summer of 1860 due to the lack of success of Charles Lever's serial *A Day's Ride*, but when *Great Expectations* began to appear circulation improved, and sales settled down to about 100 000 copies a week.

The popularity of *Great Expectations* is revealed not only in the circulation figures of *All The Year Round*, however, but in the number, size and kinds of editions which soon appeared in book form. In England Chapman and Hall's publication of the novel in three volumes went into five editions within a year, and since many of these copies were sold to circulating libraries they would, of course, be read many times over. The book was also published in Europe in Tauchnitz's *Series of English Writers*, serialised in *Harper's Weekly* magazine in America, and published in four different book-versions there; and cheaper editions of the novel soon appeared in England, such as the Library Edition of 1862 selling at 7/6d, and the Cheap Edition of 1863 selling at 3/6d.

Despite the obvious success of the novel, the reception of *Great Expectations* by the critics was more mixed. *The Times*, which had ignored Dickens's previous novels, *Bleak House, Hard Times, Little Dorrit* and *A Tale of Two Cities*, gave it a generally favourable review, praising the novel for containing more of Dickens's 'earlier fancies than we have had for years'. a point made by other critics who compared Pip enthusiastically with the hero of *David Copperfield*. *The Times*' reviewer, E. S. Dallas, was not wholly laudatory, however, for he disliked the portrait of Miss Havisham, and said that the book had other unspecified faults 'in abundance'. Nevertheless his praise is quite firm; *Great Expectations* may not be Dickens's best work, 'but it is to be ranked among his happiest', he says.

Edwin Whipple in *The Atlantic Monthly* was even more enthusiastic, particularly praising the plot, saying, 'In no other of his romances has the author succeeded so perfectly in at once stimulating and baffling the curiosity of his readers.' More than that, however, Whipple praises the novel for showing the individuality of Dickens's genius, for he says that Dickens is not a mere looker-on, an observer like Thackeray, and indeed that he lacks Thackeray's realism. But, Whipple says, Dickens used his observation as material for the creative faculties to work upon in order to show insights into real life. While many critics were worried about Dickens's apparent lack of surface realism, Whipple's review represents a genuine attempt to grapple with the problem of how Dickens's imaginative fiction is somehow more true to life than more superficially realistic novels.

Sympathetic reviews of *Great Expectations* were also carried by *The British Quarterly Review* (January, 1862) and *The Saturday Review*. The latter, which had regularly attacked Dickens in the 1850s, welcomed *Great Expectations* in July 1861 as a return to Dickens's best vein, calling it 'new, original, powerful and very entertaining', worthy to stand beside *Martin Chuzzlewit* and *David Copperfield*.

If those who liked *Great Expectations* tended to praise it because it reminded them of the hero and the humour of Dickens's earlier works, this friendly reception was far from unanimous. The *Rambler* (January, 1862), for example, found the story as 'exaggerated and impossible' as any Dickens ever wrote, and full of repetitions it called 'tedious'. Wemmick was singled out for praise 'worthy of Dickens's happiest days', but the feeling that Dickens was well past his best is clearly suggested in the hope that if Dickens would rest for a year or two, readers might not despair of seeing him produce work as good as that 'with which he charmed them a quarter of a century ago'.

The most trenchant criticism of all, however, came from Mrs Margaret Oliphant, herself a practising novelist, who called *Great Expectations* 'feeble, fatigued, and colourless', in *Blackwood's Magazine* in May, 1862. Though she praised the characters of Joe Gargery and the presentation of the convicts, Mrs Oliphant pronounced Miss Havisham and Mr Wemmick decided failures, 'specimens of oddity run mad'. The account of Orlick, she suggested, was only included for the purpose of filling a few additional pages, and she found the novel in general 'a very ineffective and colourless work'.

The mixed nature of this critical reception is not untypical of the way nearly all Dickens's later novels were received. Indeed the reviews of *Great Expectations* are rather more enthusiastic than for his two previous novels *Little Dorrit* and *A Tale of Two Cities*. The critical acclaim which *Pickwick Papers* and the other early novels had enjoyed began to wane in the 1840s, and by the 1850s critical opinion was often distinctly cool. *The Times* ignored his novels and the *Saturday Review* published a whole series of articles in the 1850s which attacked Dickens very strenuously.

The reasons for the change in critical attitudes are many and complicated. The emergence of Thackeray, in particular, and later the Brontës and George Eliot, gave Dickens a number of novel-writing rivals whose work·could be compared with his, sometimes to Dickens's disadvantage, especially in terms of realism and plot-construction as the Victorian readers perceived them. Secondly, the nature of Dickens's work did begin to change in the 1850s, from the time of *Bleak House* especially, and Dickens's social seriousness did disappoint many readers who had loved the humour and exuberance of his earlier works. Walter Bagehot's long review article on 'Charles Dickens' for the *National Review* (October, 1858) is a very clear expression of the anxieties of many Victorian readers about Dickens's work with its worries about the peculiarities of his prose-style, his clumsy plots, the love-elements, the use of pathos, and what Bagehot terms Dickens's 'sentimental radicalism'.

Though *Great Expectations* itself seems to have escaped much of the criticism of Dickens's later novels, it did not escape the critical reaction against almost all of Dickens's works which came about in the later decades of the nineteenth century. Thus Henry James reviewed *Our Mutual Friend* very severely in 1865, saying that 'for the last ten years it has seemed to us that Mr. Dickens has been unmistakably forcing himself', and damning him with the faintest of praise by calling him 'the greatest of superficial novelists'. Anthony Trollope was even more cutting in his *Autobiography* of 1883, criticising his characters because 'they are not human, nor are any of the characters human which Dickens has portrayed', while 'Of Dickens's style it is impossible to speak in praise.' The writer and editor Lesley Stephen probably summed up what many of the late-Victorians thought of Dickens when in 1888 he made his famous barbed remark: 'If literary fame could be safely measured by popularity with the half-educated, Dickens must claim the highest position among English novelists.'

Despite their fall in critical esteem, however, the popular appeal of Dickens's books with the common reader continued unabated. Twelve years after his death in 1870 no fewer than 4 239 000 copies of his books had been sold in England alone, while between 1900 and 1906 Chapman and Hall sold over two million copies.

The first signs of a critical revaluation of Dickens began to appear in the last years of the nineteenth century with George Gissing's *Charles Dickens: a Critical Study* in 1898, and G. K. Chesterton helped to produce the first of several books he wrote about Dickens in 1903. Substantial rehabilitation of Dickens as a major, almost Shakespearean, figure really began around the 1940s with George Orwell's essay 'Charles Dickens', which appeared in 1939, and Edmund Wilson's influential article 'Dickens:

78

The Two Scrooges' of 1941, the same year as Humphrey House's thoughtful book, *The Dickens World*.

Though *Great Expectations* was better received than many of Dickens's later novels when first published, its reputation has continued to rise too, so that it now stands very near the peak of Dickens's whole achievement. Two books on *Great Expectations* contain between them some of the best essays on the novel. *Assessing Great Expectations*, edited by Richard Lettis and William E. Morris, (San Francisco, 1960) contains work by such critics as Humphrey House, Dorothy Van Ghent and Barbara Hardy, while Norman Page's Casebook, *Hard Times, Great Expectations* and *Our Mutual Friend* (Macmillan, 1979) also contains useful material by such scholars as Richard Partlow and Martin Meisel.

Great Expectations has, in fact, become one of the most widely discussed, and most widely praised of all Dickens's novels. *The New Cambridge Bibliography of English Literature*, edited by George Watson in 1969, for example, lists over forty articles about it compared with fifteen for *A Tale of Two Cities* and twenty-two for *Our Mutual Friend*, the works which preceded and succeeded it.

Critical discussion of the novel today tends to concentrate on four areas which Dickens's Victorian readers perhaps underestimated or misunderstood. Works such as Robert Garis's *The Dickens Theatre* (O.U.P., 1965) and A. C. Coolidge's *Dickens as Serial Novelist* (Iowa, 1967) both relate Dickens's novels to the popular conventions of the time, and show how he used them to give his novels a greater unity of moral symbolism than was once appreciated. Writers such as the dramatist Bernard Shaw, whose essay on 'Charles Dickens and *Great Expectations*' appeared in 1937, and Edgar Johnson have shown how seriously Dickens explored social problems in the novel, and critics such as J. H. Hagan and Harry Stone have shown how carefully the novel is structured with its very precise plotting, the exact opposite of what many Victorians felt about the work. Critics generally have become much more sympathetic to the way Dickens tried to reconcile realism with symbolism in his novels, so that readers today, accepting novels as imaginative works of art rather than photographic documentaries, accept characters in Dickens's novels because of their force and their symbolic value rather than because they are exactly like people we might meet in real life. Perhaps the most important emphasis in recent interpretations of the novel is the high praise given Dickens's psychological insights, not only into the personality of Pip but also of such characters as Miss Havisham and Wemmick. Q. D. Leavis's essay 'How we must read *Great Expectations*' is a particularly sensitive account of Pip's psychological development in terms of guilt and social shame, to cite one particular example. Critics generally find the novel more serious and sombre, even with the revised ending, than Dickens's contemporaries did.

Most critics also agree, however, that it is impossible to talk about one aspect of the novel in isolation from other aspects because of the way the novel is so perfectly integrated. One cannot talk about Pip's development without discussing the kind of society he lived in, or without talking about the literary means Dickens used to express both. One cannot talk about plot without discussing character, and one cannot discuss either without discussing language. Most critics of *Great Expectations* therefore concur with the sentiments of one of the novel's earliest reviewers, that *Great Expectations* 'is, indeed, an artistic creation, and not a mere succession of humorous and pathetic scenes, and demonstrates that Dickens is now in his prime, and not in the decline of his great powers.' (*Atlantic Monthly*, September 1861).

REVISION QUESTIONS

1. *Great Expectations* has been described as the story of 'a snob's progress'. In the light of this comment, describe Pip's development in the novel, and suggest reasons why he normally retains the reader's sympathy.

2. Compare the parts played in *Great Expectations* by (a) Compeyson, and (b) Orlick.

3. After finishing the manuscript of *Great Expectations*, Dickens was persuaded by a friend to change the ending. Give your reasons for preferring *either* the original *or* the revised ending.

4. To what extent do you agree that Mrs Joe Gargery and Uncle Pumblechook shape Pip's character and career more than anyone else in the novel?

5. *Great Expectations* was first published in weekly instalments between December 1860 and August 1861. Describe some of the ways by which Dickens endeavours to retain his readers' interest in and understanding of the story over a long period of time.

6. 'Though the novel concentrates upon the story of Pip, we cannot ignore the way Dickens uses Pip's story to reveal complex truths about justice and injustice in Victorian England.' Discuss.

7. 'One of the most brilliant and moving devices Dickens uses in *Great Expectations* is repetition of incident.' Discuss Dickens's use of repetition in the novel, concentrating on three examples that seem to you particularly successful.

8. 'In *Great Expectations* generally, comedy is in the service of a very serious master' (Q. D. Leavis). Discuss three examples of Dickens's use of comedy for serious purposes in the novel.

9. *Great Expectations* has many of the same elements as a folk or fairy tale. Describe these elements, and discuss the ways in which Dickens modifies and uses them in his novel.

10. Discuss the ways Dickens is constantly revealing the differences between appearance and reality in *Great Expectations*.

11. Examine Dickens's use of symbolism in *Great Expectations*.

12. What arguments do you think Dickens might have used if a reader attacked *Great Expectations* for its use of implausible coincidences?

FURTHER READING

There are many different editions of the novel, but two recent ones which may be particularly recommended are the Macmillan Students' *Great Expectations*, edited with an Introduction and Notes by James Gibson, and the Penguin English Library *Great Expectations*, edited with an Introduction and Notes by Angus Calder.

Biography
There are many biographies of Dickens but two are outstanding:
A short and useful introduction to Dickens's life and work is Fielding, K. J., *Charles Dickens: a Critical Introduction* (second edn., enlarged, Longman, 1965).
Forster, John, *The Life of Charles Dickens* (revised with new material by A. J. Hoppé, 2 vols, Dent, 1966). An important account by one of Dickens's closest friends.
Johnson, Edgar, *Charles Dickens: His Tragedy and Triumph* (revised edn, Penguin, 1979). A recent biography which contains much new information.

Background
Collins, P., *Dickens and Crime* (Macmillan, 1962). Particularly good on Dickens's treatment of such matters as prisons and convicts.
Cruikshank, R. J., *Charles Dickens and Early Victorian England* (Pitman, 1949). A most readable and illustrated survey of the period.
House, H., *The Dickens World* (revised edn, O.U.P., 1942). A stimulating work dealing with Dickens's attitudes towards such topics as work, religion and politics.
Young, G. M., *Victorian England: Portrait of an Age* (second edn, O.U.P., 1964). A brief but concentrated historical survey.

Criticism
Butt, J. and Tillotson, K., *Dickens at Work* (Methuen, 1957). Particularly interesting on Dickens's notes for the novel.

Coolidge, A. C., Jr, *Charles Dickens as Serial Novelist* (Iowa, 1967). An account of the ways Dickens used various literary devices to overcome the difficulties of serial publication.

Gross, John and Pearson, Gabriel, *Dickens and the Twentieth Century* (Routledge and Kegan Paul, 1962). This contains a very readable chapter on *Great Expectations* by Christopher Ricks.

Hagan, John H., Jr, 'Structural Patterns in Dickens's *Great Expectations*', *English Literary History*, 21, 1954.

Miller, J. Hillis, *Charles Dickens: the World of his Novels* (O.U.P., 1958).

Leavis, F. R. and Q. D., *Dickens the Novelist* (Chatto and Windus, 1970). Chapter 6 of this difficult but important book deals with *Great Expectations*.

Lettis, Richard and Morris, William E. (eds), *Assessing Great Expectations*, (San Francisco, 1960). A collection of essays on the novel by a number of critics including Dorothy Van Ghent and Barbara Hardy.

Page, Norman (ed.), *A Casebook: Dickens: Hard Times, Great Expectations and Our Mutual Friend* (Macmillan, 1979).

Stone, Harry, *Dickens and the Invisible World: Fairy Tales, Fantasy, and Novel-Making* (Macmillan, 1979). A stimulating account of the way Dickens's novels often derive from fairy tale plots as well as personal experiences.

Thomas, R. G., *Great Expectations* (Arnold, 1964).